2nd EDITION

Ventures 1

STUDENT'S BOOK

Gretchen Bitterlin   Dennis Johnson   Donna Price   Sylvia Ramirez

K. Lynn Savage (Series Editor)

CAMBRIDGE
UNIVERSITY PRESS

CAMBRIDGE
UNIVERSITY PRESS

32 Avenue of the Americas, New York, NY 10013-2473, USA

Cambridge University Press is part of the University of Cambridge.

It furthers the University's mission by disseminating knowledge in the pursuit of education, learning and research at the highest international levels of excellence.

www.cambridge.org
Information on this title: www.cambridge.org/9781107692893

© Cambridge University Press 2014

First published 2008
6th printing 2015

Printed in Mexico by Editorial Impresora Apolo S.A de C.V.

A catalog record for this publication is available from the British Library.

ISBN 978-1-107-69289-3 Student's Book with Audio CD
ISBN 978-1-107-62859-5 Workbook with Audio CD
ISBN 978-1-139-89720-4 Online Workbook
ISBN 978-1-107-67904-7 Teacher's Edition with Assessment Audio CD / CD-ROM
ISBN 978-1-107-61822-0 Class Audio CDs
ISBN 978-1-107-65841-7 Presentation Plus

Additional resources for this publication at www.cambridge.org/ventures

Art direction, book design, photo research, and layout services: Q2A / Bill Smith
Audio production: CityVox, LLC

Authors' acknowledgments

The authors would like to acknowledge and thank focus group participants and reviewers for their insightful comments, as well as Cambridge University Press editorial, marketing, and production staffs, whose thorough research and attention to detail have resulted in a quality product.

The publishers would also like to extend their particular thanks to the following reviewers and consultants for their valuable insights and suggestions:

Kit Bell, LAUSD division of Adult and Career Education, Los Angeles, CA; **Bethany Bogage**, San Diego Community College District, San Diego, CA; **Leslie Keaton Boyd**, Dallas ISD, Dallas, TX; **Barbara Brodsky**, Teaching Work Readiness English for Refugees – Lutheran Family Services, Omaha, NE; **Jessica Buchsbaum**, City College of San Francisco, San Francisco, CA; **Helen Butner**, University of the Fraser Valley, British Columbia, Canada; **Sharon Churchill Roe**, Acadia University, Wolfville, NS, Canada; **Lisa Dolehide**, San Mateo Adult School, San Mateo, CA; **Yadira M. Dominguez**, Dallas ISD, Dallas, TX; **Donna M. Douglas**, College of DuPage, Glen Ellyn, IL; **Latarsha Dykes**, Broward Collge, Pembroke Pines, FL; **Megan L. Ernst**, Glendale Community College, Glendale, CA; **Megan Esler**, Portland Community College, Portland, OR; **Jennifer Fadden**, Fairfax County Public Schools, Fairfax, VA; **Fotine Fahouris**, College of Marin, Kentfield, CA; **Lynn Francis, M.A, M.S.**, San Diego Community College, San Diego, CA; **Danielle Gines**, Tarrant County College, Arlington, TX; **Katherine Hayne**, College of Marin, Kentfield, CA; **Armenuhi Hovhannes**, City College of San Francisco, San Francisco, CA; **Fayne B. Johnson**; **Martha L. Koranda**, College of DuPage, Glen Ellyn, IL; **Daphne Lagios**, San Mateo Adult School, San Mateo, CA; **Judy Langelier**, School District of Palm Beach County, Wellington, FL; **Janet Les**, Chilliwack Community Services, Chilliwack, British Columbia, Canada; **Keila Louzada**, Northern Virginia Community College, Sterling, VA; **Karen Mauer**, Fort Worth ISD, Fort Worth, TX; **Silvana Mehner**, Northern Virginia Community College, Sterling, VA; **Astrid T. Mendez-Gines,** Tarrant County College, Arlington, TX; **Beverly A. Miller**, Houston Community College, Houston, TX; **José Montes, MS. Ed.,** The English Center, Miami-Dade County Public Schools, Miami, FL; **Suzi Monti**, Community College of Baltimore County, Baltimore, MD; **Irina Morgunova**, Roxbury Community College, Roxbury Crossing, MA; **Julia Morgunova**, Roxbury Community College, Roxbury Crossing, MA; **Susan Otero**, Fairfax County Public Schools, Fairfax, VA; **Sergei Paromchik**, Hillsborough County Public Schools, Tampa, FL; **Pearl W. Pigott**, Houston Community College, Houston, TX; **Marlene Ramirez**, The English Center, Miami-Dade County Public Schools, Miami, FL; **Cory Rayala**, Harbor Service Center, LAUSD, Los Angeles, CA; **Catherine M. Rifkin**, Florida State College at Jacksonville, Jacksonville, FL; **Danette Roe**, Evans Community Adult School, Los Angeles, CA; **Maria Roy**, Kilgore College, Kilgore, TX; **Jill Shalongo**, Glendale Community College, Glendale, CA, and Sierra Linda High School, Phoenix, AZ; **Laurel Owensby Slater**, San Diego Community College District, San Diego, CA; **Rheba Smith**, San Diego Community College District, San Diego, CA; **Jennifer Snyder**, Portland Community College, Portland, OR; **Mary K. Solberg**, Metropolitan Community College, Omaha, NE; **Rosanne Vitola**, Austin Community College, Austin, TX

Scope and sequence

UNIT TITLE TOPIC	FUNCTIONS	LISTENING AND SPEAKING	VOCABULARY	GRAMMAR FOCUS
Welcome pages 2–5	■ Identifying the letters of the alphabet ■ Identifying numbers ■ Identifying days and months ■ Identifying abbreviations	■ Saying the alphabet and numbers ■ Spelling numbers and names ■ Saying days and months ■ Saying your birth month	■ The alphabet with capital and lowercase letters ■ Numbers ■ Months and days	
Unit 1 **Personal information** pages 6–17 Topic: **Introductions**	■ Identifying names ■ Identifying numbers ■ Using greetings ■ Identifying countries of origin ■ Exchanging personal information	■ Clarifying spelling ■ Using greetings ■ Using appropriate language to introduce self and others	■ Personal information ■ Countries and nationalities ■ Personal titles	■ Possessive adjectives ■ Subject pronouns ■ Simple present of *be* ■ Contractions
Unit 2 **At school** pages 18–29 Topic: **The classroom**	■ Describing location ■ Finding out location	■ Asking and giving location of things ■ Saying *excuse me*	■ Classroom furniture ■ Classroom objects	■ Prepositions of location (*in, on, under*) ■ *Where is?* ■ Singular and plural nouns ■ *Yes / No* questions ■ *This / that* and *these / those* ■ Contractions
Review: Units 1 and 2 pages 30–31		■ Understanding a conversation		
Unit 3 **Friends and family** pages 32–43 Topic: **Family**	■ Describing actions ■ Talking about family members	■ Asking and answering questions about current activities ■ Answering questions about your family	■ Family relationships ■ Daily activities ■ Descriptive adjectives	■ Present continuous ■ *Wh-* questions ■ *Yes / No* questions ■ Object pronouns (*him, her, it, them*)
Unit 4 **Health** pages 44–55 Topic: **Health problems**	■ Describing health problems and suggesting remedies ■ Expressing sympathy	■ Asking about someone's health ■ Expressing sympathy ■ Suggesting a remedy	■ Body parts ■ Health problems ■ Descriptive adjectives	■ Simple present of *have* ■ Questions with *have* ■ *have* and *need* ■ Contractions
Review: Units 3 and 4 pages 56–57		■ Understanding a narrative		
Unit 5 **Around town** pages 58–69 Topic: **Places and directions**	■ Describing location ■ Giving directions ■ Asking for directions ■ Confirming by repetition	■ Asking about a location ■ Describing your neighborhood ■ Clarifying directions	■ Building and place names ■ Imperatives for directions	■ Prepositions of location (*on, next to, across from, between, on the corner of*) ■ *Where* questions ■ Affirmative and negative imperatives

READING	WRITING	LIFE SKILLS	PRONUNCIATION
■ Reading the alphabet ■ Reading numbers ■ Reading months and days	■ Writing the alphabet ■ Writing names ■ Writing numbers ■ Writing days	■ Understanding dates	■ Pronouncing the alphabet ■ Pronouncing numbers ■ Pronouncing days and months
■ Reading a paragraph describing a student's personal information	■ Writing sentences giving personal information ■ Identifying and using capital letters	■ Reading a registration form ■ Understanding cultural differences in names ■ Using personal titles ■ Using a directory ■ Reading an ID card	■ Pronouncing key vocabulary ■ Saying telephone numbers ■ Saying addresses
■ Reading sentences describing a classroom ■ Using pictorial cues	■ Writing sentences about the location of items in the classroom ■ Using capitalization and periods	■ Reading an inventory list ■ Counting objects	■ Pronouncing key vocabulary
			■ Recognizing syllables
■ Reading a paragraph describing a family birthday party ■ Using a passage's title for comprehension	■ Writing sentences about your own family ■ Writing number words	■ Reading an insurance application form ■ Using family trees ■ Using formal and informal family titles	■ Pronouncing key vocabulary
■ Reading a paragraph describing a sick family's visit to a doctor's office ■ Interpreting exclamation points	■ Writing an absence note to a child's teacher ■ Writing dates	■ Using an appointment card ■ Matching remedies to ailments ■ Showing concern for someone's health	■ Pronouncing key vocabulary
			■ Pronouncing strong syllables
■ Reading an e-mail describing a neighborhood ■ Interpreting pronoun referents	■ Writing a description of your neighborhood ■ Capitalizing proper nouns	■ Reading and drawing maps ■ Giving and getting directions ■ Understanding what a DMV is	■ Pronouncing key vocabulary

UNIT TITLE TOPIC	FUNCTIONS	LISTENING AND SPEAKING	VOCABULARY	GRAMMAR FOCUS
Unit 6 **Time** pages 70–81 Topic: **Daily activities and time**	▪ Describing habitual activities ▪ Asking for dates and times ▪ Giving information about dates and times	▪ Using *usually* vs. *always* ▪ Using *has* vs. *goes to* for classes ▪ Talking about daily schedules	▪ Times of the day ▪ Habitual activities	▪ Simple present tense ▪ *Wh-* questions ▪ Prepositions of time (*at*, *in*, *on*) ▪ *start / end* and *open / close*
Review: Units 5 and 6 pages 82–83		▪ Understanding a conversation		
Unit 7 **Shopping** pages 84–95 Topic: **Food and money**	▪ Asking about quantity ▪ Reading prices ▪ Asking the location of items	▪ Asking and answering *How many?* and *How much?* ▪ Talking about what there is and isn't ▪ Using quantifiers	▪ Grocery store items ▪ U.S. currency	▪ Count and non-count nouns ▪ *How many? / How much?* ▪ *There is / There are* ▪ Quantifiers with non-count nouns ▪ *some* and *any*
Unit 8 **Work** pages 96–107 Topic: **Jobs and skills**	▪ Identifying past and present jobs ▪ Describing skills	▪ Talking about your job ▪ Talking about skills	▪ Occupations ▪ Work locations	▪ Simple past of *be* (statements and questions) ▪ *Can* ▪ Contractions ▪ *be* with *and* and *but*
Review: Units 7 and 8 pages 108–109		▪ Understanding a narrative		
Unit 9 **Daily living** pages 110–121 Topic: **Home responsibilities**	▪ Describing past actions ▪ Discussing chores ▪ Expressing appreciation	▪ Talking about household activities	▪ Chores ▪ Household items ▪ Time words	▪ Simple past tense of regular and irregular verbs ▪ *Or* questions
Unit 10 **Free time** pages 122–133 Topic: **Free-time activities**	▪ Describing past actions ▪ Describing future actions ▪ Discussing plans	▪ Talking about free-time activities	▪ Free-time activities ▪ Sports	▪ Simple past of irregular verbs ▪ Future with *be going to* ▪ Contrasting past, present, and future
Review: Units 9 and 10 pages 134–135		▪ Understanding a conversation		

READING	WRITING	LIFE SKILLS	PRONUNCIATION
■ Reading a paragraph describing a person's schedule ■ Using *Wh-* questions to interpret a reading	■ Writing a description of your schedule ■ Using indents for paragraphs	■ Using class and other schedules ■ Understanding Parent-Teacher Associations ■ Understanding volunteerism ■ Using calendars ■ Reading clocks	■ Pronouncing key vocabulary
			■ Understanding intonation in questions
■ Reading a paragraph describing a shopping trip ■ Looking for clues to understand new words	■ Writing a note about a shopping list ■ Using commas in a list	■ Reading supermarket ads ■ Reading receipts and using basic consumer math ■ Using U.S. currency ■ Using multiple payment methods	■ Pronouncing key vocabulary
■ Reading a letter describing a person's job and work history ■ Interpreting narrative time through verb tense	■ Writing a paragraph about your skills ■ Checking spelling	■ Completing job applications ■ Identifying skills ■ Understanding job certification ■ Reading e-mail	■ Pronouncing key vocabulary
			■ Pronouncing the *-s* ending with plural nouns
■ Reading a letter describing daily events ■ Interpreting the narrative voice	■ Writing a letter describing household chores ■ Using the simple past in writing	■ Using a job-duties chart ■ Understanding household chores and tools used for them	■ Pronouncing key vocabulary
■ Reading an e-mail and a letter describing a vacation ■ Interpreting time words in a passage	■ Writing a letter describing a past and future vacation ■ Creating new paragraphs as the tense changes	■ Reading a TV schedule ■ Using schedules ■ Understanding the cultural features of sports	■ Pronouncing key vocabulary
			■ Pronouncing the *-ed* ending in the simple past

To the teacher

What is *Ventures*?

Ventures is a six-level, four-skills, standards-based, integrated-skills series that empowers students to achieve their academic and career goals.

- This most complete program with a wealth of resources provides instructors with the tools for any teaching situation.
- The new Online Workbook keeps students learning outside the classroom.
- Easy-to-teach materials make for a more productive classroom.

What components does *Ventures* have?

Student's Book with Audio CD

Each of the core **Student's Books** contains ten topic-focused units, interspersed with five review units. The main units feature six skill-focused lessons.

- **Lessons** in the Student's Book are self-contained, allowing for completion within a one-hour class period.
- **Review lessons** recycle and reinforce the listening, vocabulary, and grammar skills developed in the two prior units and include a pronunciation activity.
- **Self-assessments** in the back of the book give students an opportunity to reflect on their learning. They support learner persistence and help determine whether students are ready for the unit test.
- **Reference charts**, also in the back of the book, provide grammar paradigms; rules for spelling, punctuation, and grammar; and lists of ordinal numbers, cardinal numbers, countries, and nationalities.
- References to the **Self-study audio CD** that accompanies the Student's Book are indicated in the Student's Book by an icon and track number: Look for the audio icon and track number to find activities with self-study audio. "STUDENT" refers to the self-study audio, and "CLASS" refers to the class audio. A full class audio is available separately.

  STUDENT TK 10
  CLASS CD1 TK 14

- A **Student Arcade,** available online at www.cambridge.org/venturesarcade, allows students to practice their skills with interactive activities and download self-study audio.

Teacher's Edition with Assessment Audio CD / CD-ROM

The interleaved **Teacher's Edition** includes easy-to-follow lesson plans for every unit.

- Tips and suggestions address common areas of difficulty for students and provide suggestions for expansion activities and improving learner persistence.
- A **More Ventures** chart at the end of each lesson indicates where to find additional practice material in other *Ventures* components such as the Workbook, Online Teacher's Resource Room (see below), and Student Arcade.
- Unit, midterm, and final tests, which include listening, vocabulary, grammar, reading, and writing sections, are found in the back of the Teacher's Edition.
- The **Assessment Audio CD / CD-ROM** that accompanies the Teacher's Edition contains the audio for each unit, midterm, and final test. It also features all the tests in customizable format so teachers can customize them to suit their needs.

Online Teacher's Resource Room (www.cambridge.org/myresourceroom)

Ventures 2nd Edition offers a free Online Teacher's Resource Room where teachers can download hundreds of additional worksheets and classroom materials including:

- A *placement test* that helps place students into appropriate levels of *Ventures*.
- A *Career and Educational Pathways* solution that helps students identify their educational and career goals.
- *Collaborative activities* for each lesson in Levels 1–4 that develop cooperative learning and community building within the classroom.
- *Writing worksheets* that help Literacy-level students recognize and write shapes, letters, and numbers, while alphabet and number cards promote partner and group work.
- *Picture dictionary cards and worksheets* that reinforce vocabulary learned in Levels Basic, 1, and 2.
- *Extended readings and worksheets* that provide added reading skills development for Levels 3 and 4.
- *Add Ventures* worksheets that were designed for use in multilevel classrooms and in leveled classes where the proficiency level of students differs.

Log on to www.cambridge.org/myresourceroom to explore these and hundreds of other free resources.

Workbook with Audio CD

The **Workbook** provides two pages of activities for each lesson in the Student's Book and includes an audio CD.

- If used in class, the Workbook can extend classroom instructional time by 30 minutes per lesson.
- The exercises are designed so learners can complete them in class or independently. Students can check their answers with the answer key in the back of the Workbook. Workbook exercises can be assigned in class, for homework, or as student support when a class is missed.
- Grammar charts at the back of the Workbook allow students to use the Workbook for self-study.

Online Workbooks

The self-grading **Online Workbooks** offer programs the flexibility of introducing blended learning.

- They provide the same high-quality practice opportunities as the print Workbooks and give students instant feedback.
- They allow teachers and programs to track student progress and time on task.

Unit organization

Each unit has six skill-focused lessons:

LESSON A Listening focuses students on the unit topic. The initial exercise, **Before you listen**, creates student interest with visuals that help the teacher assess what learners already know and serve as a prompt for the unit's key vocabulary. Next is **Listen**, which is based on conversations. Students relate vocabulary to meaning and relate the spoken and written forms of new theme-related vocabulary. **After you listen** concludes the lesson by practicing language related to the theme in a communicative activity, either orally with a partner or individually in a writing activity.

LESSONS B AND C focus on grammar. The lessons move from a **Grammar focus** that presents the grammar point in chart form; to **Practice** exercises that check comprehension of the grammar point and provide guided practice; and, finally, to **Communicate** exercises that guide learners as they generate original answers and

conversations. These lessons often include a *Culture note*, which provides information directly related to the conversation practice (such as the use of titles with last names), or a *Useful language* note, which introduces useful expressions and functional language.

LESSON D Reading develops reading skills and expands vocabulary. The lesson opens with a **Before you read** exercise, designed to activate prior knowledge and encourage learners to make predictions. A *Reading tip*, which focuses on a specific reading skill, accompanies the **Read** exercise. The reading section of the lesson concludes with **After you read** exercises that check comprehension. In Levels Basic, 1, and 2, the vocabulary expansion portion of the lesson is a **Picture dictionary**. It includes a *word bank*, pictures to identify, and a conversation for practicing the new words. The words expand vocabulary related to the unit topic. In Books 3 and 4, the vocabulary expansion portion of the lesson uses new vocabulary from the reading to build skills such as recognizing word families, selecting definitions based on the context of the reading, and using clues in the reading to guess meaning.

LESSON E Writing provides practice with process writing within the context of the unit. **Before you write** exercises provide warm-up activities to activate the language needed for the writing assignment, followed by one or more exercises that provide a model for students to follow when they write. A *Writing tip* presents information about punctuation or paragraph organization directly related to the writing assignment. The **Write** exercise sets goals for the student writing. In the **After you write** exercise, students share with a partner.

LESSON F Another view has three sections. **Life-skills reading** develops the scanning and skimming skills used with documents such as forms, charts, schedules, announcements, and ads. Multiple-choice questions (modeled on CASAS[1] and BEST[2]) develop test-taking skills. **Grammar connections**, in Levels 1–4, contrasts grammar points and includes guided practice and communicative activities. Finally, **Wrap up** refers students to the self-assessment page in the back of the book, where they can check their knowledge and evaluate their progress.

---

[1] The Comprehensive Adult Student Assessment System. For more information, see www.casas.org.
[2] The Basic English Skills Test. For more information, see www.cal.org/BEST.

Unit tour

The Most Complete Course for Student Success

Ventures empowers students to achieve their academic and career goals.

- The most complete program with a wealth of resources provides instructors with the tools for any teaching situation.
- The new Online Workbook keeps students learning outside the classroom.
- Easy-to-teach materials make for a more productive classroom.

The Big Picture

- Introduces the unit topic and provides rich opportunities for classroom discussion.
- Activates students' prior knowledge and previews the unit vocabulary.

Unit Goals

- Explicit unit goals ensure student involvement in the learning process.

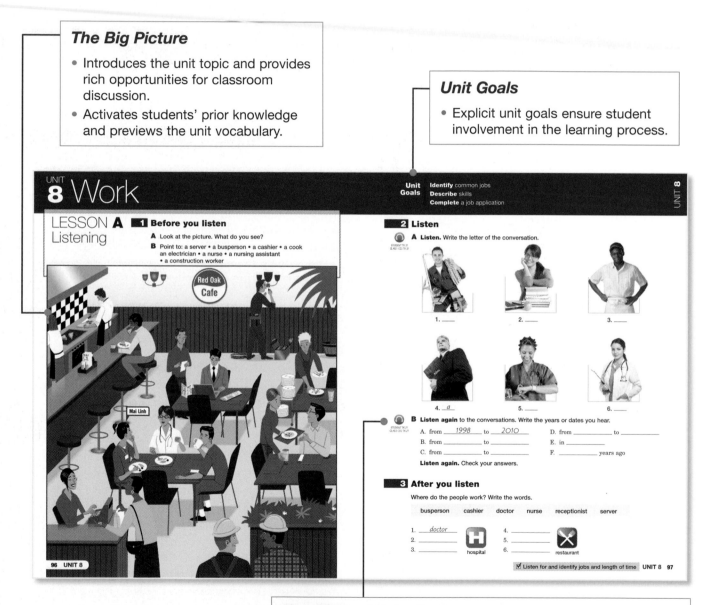

Two Different Audio Programs

- Class audio features over 100 minutes of listening practice to improve listening comprehension.
- Self-study audio encourages learner persistence and autonomy.
- Easy navigation between the two with clear track listings.

Grammar Chart

- Clear grammar charts with additional grammar reference in the back of the book allow for greater teacher flexibility.

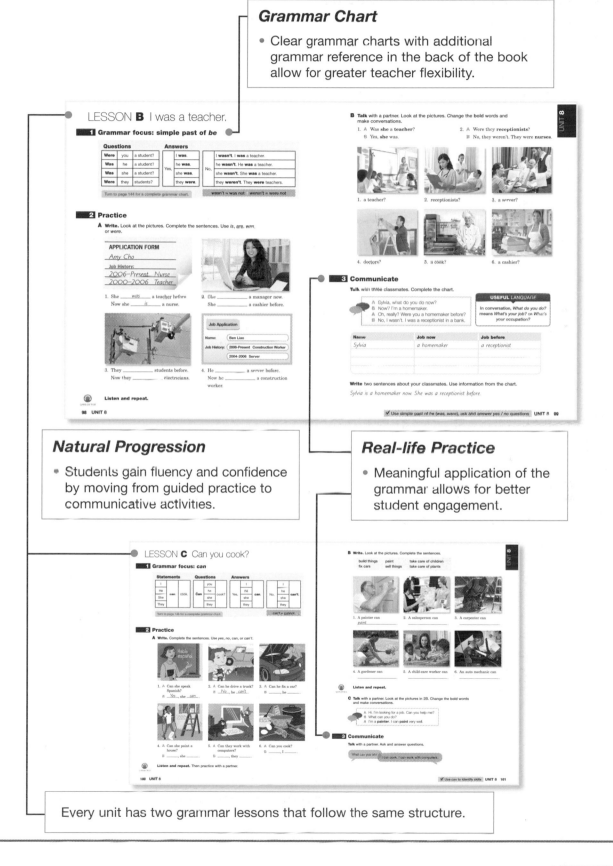

Natural Progression

- Students gain fluency and confidence by moving from guided practice to communicative activities.

Real-life Practice

- Meaningful application of the grammar allows for better student engagement.

Every unit has two grammar lessons that follow the same structure.

Reading

- *Ventures* features a three-step reading approach that highlights reading strategies and skills needed for success: **Before you read, Read, After you read.**

Integrated-skills Approach

- Reading is combined with writing and listening for an integrated approach that ensures better comprehension.

Picture Dictionary

- This visual page expands unit vocabulary and works on pronunciation for richer understanding of the topic.

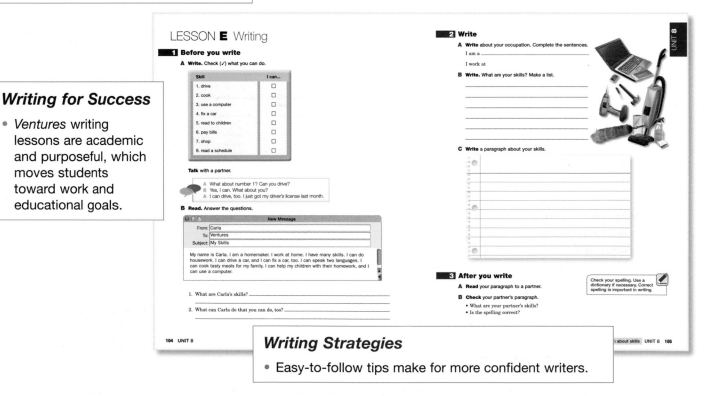

Process Writing

- *Ventures* includes a robust process-writing approach: prewriting, writing, and peer review.

Talk with a Partner

- Spoken practice helps students internalize the vocabulary and relate it to their lives.

Writing for Success

- *Ventures* writing lessons are academic and purposeful, which moves students toward work and educational goals.

Writing Strategies

- Easy-to-follow tips make for more confident writers.

Document Literacy

- Explicit practice with authentic-type documents builds real-life skills.

Grammar Connections

- Contrasting two grammar forms in a communicative way helps with grammar accuracy.

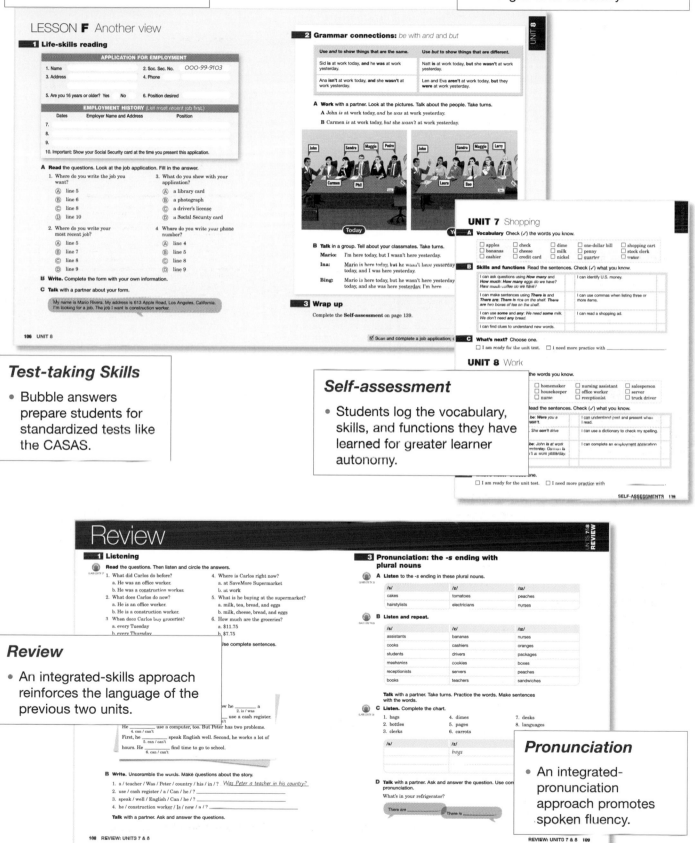

Test-taking Skills

- Bubble answers prepare students for standardized tests like the CASAS.

Self-assessment

- Students log the vocabulary, skills, and functions they have learned for greater learner autonomy.

Review

- An integrated-skills approach reinforces the language of the previous two units.

Pronunciation

- An integrated-pronunciation approach promotes spoken fluency.

Correlations

UNIT	CASAS Competencies	NRS Educational Functioning Level Descriptors *Oral BEST: 16–28 (SPL 2)* *BEST Plus: 401–417 (SPL 2)* *BEST Literacy: 8–35 (SPL 2)*
Unit 1 **Personal information** Pages 6–17	0.1.2, 0.1.3, 0.1.4, 0.1.5, 0.1.6, 0.2.1, 0.2.2, 2.1.1, 2.1.8, 2.4.1, 2.5.5, 2.7.2, 4.8.1, 6.0.1, 7.2.4, 7.4.3, 7.5.6	▪ Basic greetings and phrases ▪ Answering personal information questions ▪ Reading numbers and letters ▪ Reading common sight words ▪ Writing familiar words ▪ Providing information on forms ▪ Writing basic personal information
Unit 2 **At school** Pages 18–29	0.1.2, 0.1.4, 0.1.5, 2.5.5, 4.5.3, 4.6.2, 4.6.5, 4.7.2, 4.7.4, 4.8.1, 6.0.1, 6.0.2, 6.1.1, 7.1.4, 7.4.5	▪ Basic greetings and phrases ▪ Answering common questions´ ▪ Reading numbers and letters ▪ Reading common sight words ▪ Writing familiar words ▪ Recognizing forms at home, work, and in the community ▪ Exposure to computers or technology
Unit 3 **Friends and family** Pages 32–43	0.1.2, 0.1.4, 0.1.8, 0.2.1, 0.2.4, 1.4.1, 2.6.1, 2.7.1, 2.7.2, 6.0.1, 6.0.2, 7.1.4, 7.2.4, 7.4.7, 7.4.8, 7.5.6, 8.1.3, 8.2.1, 8.3.1	▪ Basic greetings and phrases ▪ Answering common questions ▪ Answering personal information questions ▪ Reading numbers and letters ▪ Reading common sight words ▪ Writing familiar words ▪ Providing information on forms
Unit 4 **Health** Pages 44–55	0.1.1, 0.1.2, 0.1.3, 0.1.4, 0.2.1, 0.2.3, 2.1.8, 2.3.2, 2.5.3, 2.5.5, 3.1.1, 3.1.2, 3.1.3, 3.2.1, 3.2.3, 3.3.1, 3.4.1, 3.4.3, 3.5.7, 4.6.1, 4.8.1, 6.0.1, 7.2.2, 7.2.4, 7.2.6, 7.3.2, 7.5.5, 7.5.6	▪ Basic greetings and phrases ▪ Answering personal information questions ▪ Communicating immediate needs ▪ Reading numbers and letters ▪ Reading common sight words ▪ Writing familiar words ▪ Recognizing forms at home, work, and in the community

All units of *Ventures 2nd Edition* meet most of the EFF content standards and provide overall BEST test preparation.

The chart above lists areas of particular focus.

For more details and correlations to other state standards, go to: www.cambridge.org/myresourceroom

EFF	Florida Adult ESOL Low Beginning	LAUSD ESL Beginning Low Competencies
▪ Conveying ideas in writing ▪ Listening actively ▪ Practicing lifelong learning skills ▪ Reading with understanding ▪ Seeking feedback and revising accordingly ▪ Speaking so others can understand ▪ Testing learning in real-life applications ▪ Understanding and working with numbers ▪ Cooperating with others	2.01.01, 2.01.02, 2.01.03, 2.01.04, 2.03.12, 2.03.16	I. 1, 2, 4, 5, 7 II. 9, 11 III. 16, 26 V. 40 VIII. 58a, 58b, 58c
▪ Assessing the needs of others ▪ Attending to visual sources of information ▪ Interacting with others in positive ways ▪ Offering input ▪ Organizing and presenting information ▪ Seeking feedback and revising accordingly ▪ Understanding and working with numbers ▪ Cooperating with others ▪ Speaking so others can understand	2.01.02, 2.01.04, 2.03.12, 2.03.16, 2.04.01	I. 1 II. 9 III. 15
▪ Cooperating with others ▪ Listening actively ▪ Making inferences, predictions, or judgments ▪ Monitoring comprehension ▪ Organizing and relaying information effectively ▪ Paying attention to the conventions of the English language ▪ Seeking feedback and revising accordingly ▪ Speaking so others can understand	2.01.01, 2.01.02, 2.01.03, 2.01.04, 2.01.05, 2.01.06, 2.03.12, 2.03.16, 2.04.01, 2.05.01, 2.05.02	I. 3, 6, 7 II. 12, 13 III. 19 IV. 38
▪ Anticipating and identifying problems ▪ Attending to oral communication ▪ Defining what one is trying to achieve ▪ Gathering facts and supporting information ▪ Organizing and relaying spoken information effectively ▪ Selecting appropriate reading strategies ▪ Taking responsibility for learning ▪ Cooperating with others ▪ Speaking so others can understand	2.01.02, 2.01.03, 2.01.04, 2.01.05, 2.01.09, 2.01.10, 2.02.02, 2.03.12, 2.03.16, 2.04.09, 2.06.03	IV. 43, 44 VI. 44 VII. 57

UNIT	CASAS Competencies	NRS Educational Functioning Level Descriptors *Oral BEST: 16–28 (SPL 2)* *BEST Plus: 401–417 (SPL 2)* *BEST Literacy: 8–35 (SPL 2)*
Unit 5 **Around town** Pages 58–69	0.1.1, 0.1.2, 0.1.3, 0.1.4, 0.2.1, 0.2.3, 1.1.3, 1.3.7, 1.4.1, 1.9.2, 1.9.4, 2.2.1, 2.2.3, 2.2.5, 2.5.4, 2.6.3, 4.8.1, 5.2.4, 6.0.1, 6.6.5, 7.1.2, 7.1.4, 7.2.2, 7.2.4, 7.2.7, 7.3.2, 7.3.4, 7.4.8, 7.5.6, 8.3.2	▪ Basic greetings and phrases ▪ Answering common questions ▪ Answering personal information questions ▪ Reading numbers and letters ▪ Writing familiar words ▪ Writing basic personal information ▪ Exposure to computers or technology
Unit 6 **Time** Pages 70–81	0.1.2, 0.1.4, 0.2.4, 2.3.1, 2.3.2, 2.5.5, 2.6.1, 2.6.3, 2.7.1, 4.1.6, 4.1.7, 4.2.1, 4.3.1, 6.0.1, 6.0.3, 7.1.2, 7.1.4, 7.2.4, 8.1.1, 8.1.2, 8.1.3	▪ Basic greetings and phrases ▪ Answering common questions ▪ Answering personal information questions ▪ Reading numbers and letters ▪ Reading common sight words ▪ Writing familiar words ▪ Writing basic personal information
Unit 7 **Shopping** Pages 84–95	0.1.2, 0.2.4, 1.1.6, 1.1.7, 1.2.1, 1.2.2, 1.2.5, 1.3.1, 1.3.6, 1.3.8, 1.5.1, 1.5.3, 1.6.4, 1.8.1, 1.8.2, 2.6.4, 6.0.1, 6.0.2, 6.0.3, 6.0.4, 6.1.1, 6.1.2, 6.2.1, 6.2.2, 6.2.5, 6.5.1, 6.6.7, 6.9.2, 7.1.3, 7.1.4, 7.2.3, 7.5.6, 8.2.1	▪ Basic greetings and phrases ▪ Answering common questions ▪ Communicating immediate needs ▪ Reading numbers and letters ▪ Reading common sight words ▪ Writing familiar words ▪ Recognizing forms at home, work, and in the community
Unit 8 **Work** Pages 96–107	0.1.2, 0.2.1, 0.2.2, 1.9.6, 4.1.1, 4.1.2, 4.1.5, 4.1.6, 4.1.8, 4.4.2, 4.4.4, 4.4.7, 4.5.1, 4.6.2, 7.1.1, 7.1.4, 7.2.3, 7.2.4, 7.5.1, 7.5.6, 8.2.1, 8.2.6	▪ Basic greetings and phrases ▪ Answering personal information questions ▪ Writing familiar words ▪ Writing basic personal information ▪ Completing simple forms ▪ Providing information on forms ▪ Exposure to computers or technology
Unit 9 **Daily living** Pages 110–121	0.1.2, 0.2.4, 1.4.1, 1.7.4, 2.3.2, 4.6.3, 7.1.4, 7.2.2, 7.4.8, 7.5.1, 7.5.5, 8.1.1, 8.1.4, 8.2.1, 8.2.2, 8.2.3, 8.2.4, 8.2.5, 8.2.6, 8.3.1	▪ Basic greetings and phrases ▪ Answering common questions ▪ Answering personal information questions ▪ Reading numbers and letters ▪ Reading common sight words ▪ Writing familiar words
Unit 10 **Free time** Pages 122–133	0.1.2, 0.1.4, 0.2.4, 2.3.2, 2.6.1, 2.6.2, 2.6.3, 5.2.4, 6.0.1, 6.0.3, 7.1.4, 7.5.1, 7.5.6	▪ Answering common questions ▪ Answering personal information questions ▪ Reading numbers and letters ▪ Reading common sight words ▪ Writing familiar words ▪ Recognizing forms at home, work, and in the community ▪ Exposure to computers or technology

All units of *Ventures 2nd Edition* meet most of the EFF content standards and provide overall BEST test preparation.

The chart above lists areas of particular focus.

For more details and correlations to other state standards, go to: www.cambridge.org/myresourceroom

EFF	Florida Adult ESOL Low Beginning	LAUSD ESL Beginning Low Competencies
■ Assessing interests, resources, and the potential for success ■ Attending to visual sources of information ■ Defining what one is trying to achieve ■ Establishing goals based on one's own current and future needs ■ Identifying and using strategies appropriate to goals and tasks ■ Organizing and relaying spoken information effectively ■ Understanding, interpreting, and working with symbolic information ■ Cooperating with others ■ Speaking so others can understand	2.01.04, 2.01.10, 2.02.01, 2.02.02, 2.03.12, 2.03.16, 2.04.09, 2.06.02, 2.06.03	I. 2 II. 9, 11 III. 17, 23 V. 42 VI. 49
■ Attending to visual sources of information ■ Communicating using a variety of mathematical representations ■ Paying attention to the conventions of spoken English ■ Setting and prioritizing goals ■ Understanding, interpreting, and working with numbers and symbolic information ■ Cooperating with others ■ Speaking so others can understand	2.01.04, 2.01.05, 2.01.10, 2.02.09, 2.02.10, 2.03.12	II. 12, 13 III. 16, 22, 23, 25, 26 VII. 55
■ Cooperating with others ■ Determining the reading purpose ■ Integrating information with prior knowledge ■ Monitoring the effectiveness of communication ■ Seeking feedback and revising accordingly ■ Speaking so others can understand ■ Using math to solve problems and communicate	2.01.04, 2.03.12, 2.04.01, 2.04.02, 2.05.06	IV. 30, 31, 35, 36 VII. 50, 51, 52
■ Conveying ideas in writing ■ Cooperating with others ■ Listening actively ■ Speaking so others can understand ■ Taking stock of where one is	2.01.02, 2.01.03, 2.01.04, 2.03.01, 2.03.02, 2.03.04, 2.03.05, 2.03.12, 2.03.13, 2.03.14, 2.03.15, 2.03.16	I. 7 II. 14 IV. 31, 35 VII. 50, 51, 54
■ Attending to visual sources of information ■ Cooperating with others ■ Integrating readings with prior knowledge ■ Monitoring the effectiveness of communication ■ Organizing and presenting written information ■ Setting and prioritizing goals ■ Speaking so others can understand	2.01.03, 2.01.04, 2.03.10, 2.03.12, 2.05.05	II. 12, 13 IV. 31, 35, 38 VII. 55
■ Determining the communication purpose ■ Interacting with others in positive ways ■ Monitoring listening comprehension ■ Reflecting and evaluating ■ Seeking feedback and revising accordingly ■ Speaking so others can understand ■ Cooperating with others	2.01.03, 2.01.04, 2.01.10, 2.02.02, 2.03.12, 2.03.16	II. 12, 13 III. 19, 22, 23 VII. 52, 54, 55

Meet the *Ventures* author team

Gretchen Bitterlin has been an ESL teacher and an ESL department chair. She is currently the ESL coordinator for the Continuing Education Program at San Diego Community College District. Under Gretchen's leadership, the ESL program has developed several products – for example, an ESL oral interview placement test and writing rubrics for assessing writing for level exit – now used by other agencies. She is a co-author of *English for Adult Competency*, has been an item writer for CASAS tests, and chaired the task force that developed the TESOL *Adult Education Program Standards*. She is a recipient of her district's award, Outstanding Contract Faculty. Gretchen holds an MA in TESOL from the University of Arizona.

Dennis Johnson had his first language-teaching experience as a Peace Corps volunteer in South Korea. Following that teaching experience, he became an in-country ESL trainer. After returning to the United States, he became an ESL trainer and began teaching credit and non-credit ESL at City College of San Francisco. As ESL site coordinator, he has provided guidance to faculty in selecting textbooks. He is the author of *Get Up and Go* and co-author of *The Immigrant Experience*. Dennis is the demonstration teacher on the *Ventures Professional Development DVD*. Dennis holds an MA in music from Stanford University.

Donna Price began her ESL career teaching EFL in Madagascar. She is currently associate professor of ESL and vocational ESL / technology resource instructor for the Continuing Education Program, San Diego Community College District. She has served as an author and a trainer for CALPRO, the California Adult Literacy Professional Development Project, co-authoring training modules on contextualizing and integrating workforce skills into the ESL classroom. She is a recipient of the TESOL Newbury House Award for Excellence in Teaching, and she is author of *Skills for Success*. Donna holds an MA in linguistics from San Diego State University.

Sylvia Ramirez started as an instructional aide in ESL. Since then she has been a part-time teacher, a full-time teacher, and a program coordinator. As program coordinator at Mira Costa College, she provided leadership in establishing Managed Enrollment, Student Learning Outcomes, and Transitioning Adults to Academic and Career Preparation. Her more than forty years in adult ESL includes multilevel ESL, vocational ESL, family literacy, and distance learning. She has also provided technical assistance to local ESL programs for the California State Department of Education. In 2011 she received the Hayward Award in education. Her MA is in education / counseling from Point Loma University, and she has certificates in TESOL and in online teaching.

K. Lynn Savage first taught English in Japan. She began teaching ESL at City College of San Francisco in 1974, where she has taught all levels of non-credit ESL and has served as vocational ESL resource teacher. She has trained teachers for adult education programs around the country as well as abroad. She chaired the committee that developed *ESL Model Standards for Adult Education Programs* (California, 1992) and is the author, co-author, and editor of many ESL materials including *Crossroads Café, Teacher Training through Video, Parenting for Academic Success, Building Life Skills, Picture Stories, May I Help You?*, and *English That Works*. Lynn holds an MA in TESOL from Teachers College, Columbia University.

To the student

Welcome to **Ventures**! The dictionary says that "venture" means a risky or daring journey. Its meaning is similar to the word "adventure." Learning English is certainly a journey and an adventure. We hope that this book helps you in your journey of learning English to fulfill your goals. We believe that this book will prepare you for academic and career courses and give you the English skills you need to get a job or promotion, go to college, or communicate better in your community. The CDs, the workbooks, and the free Internet practice on the Arcade will help you improve your English outside class. Setting your personal goals will also help. Take a few minutes and write down your goals below.

Good luck in your studies!

The Author Team
Gretchen Bitterlin
Dennis Johnson
Donna Price
Sylvia Ramirez
K. Lynn Savage

My goals for studying English

1. My first goal for studying English:	Date: _____
2. My second goal for studying English:	Date: _____
3. My third goal for studying English:	Date: _____

Welcome

1 Meet your classmates

Look at the picture. What do you see?

English level 1

Eduardo

Pierre

Kankou

Ryoko

Tariq

Ivan

Ivan

Paolo

2 The alphabet

STUDENT TK 2
CLASS CD1 TK 2

A Listen. Students are introducing themselves. Check (✓) the names you hear.

✓ Eduardo   ✓ Paolo   ✓ Ryoko

___ Pierre   ___ Tariq   ✓ Kankou

STUDENT TK 3
CLASS CD1 TK 3

B Listen and write the letters.

Aa *A a*	Bb ___	Cc ___	Dd ___	Ee ___	Ff ___	Gg ___
Hh ___	Ii ___	Jj ___	Kk ___	Ll ___	Mm ___	Nn ___
Oo ___	Pp ___	Qq ___	Rr ___	Ss ___	Tt ___	Uu ___
Vv ___	Ww ___	Xx ___	Yy ___	Zz ___		

Talk with your partner. Take turns. Say a letter. Your partner points to the letter.

STUDENT TK 4
CLASS CD1 TK 4

C Listen and repeat.

A What's your name?
B Helena.
A How do you spell that?
B H-E-L-E-N-A.

Talk to five classmates. Write the names.

Class list
Helena
1.
2.
3.
4.
5.

3 Numbers

A Listen and repeat.

0 zero	1 one	2 two	3 three	4 four	5 five
6 six	7 seven	8 eight	9 nine	10 ten
11 eleven	12 twelve	13 thirteen	14 fourteen	15 fifteen
16 sixteen	17 seventeen	18 eighteen	19 nineteen	20 twenty

Talk with a partner. Take turns. Say a number. Your partner points to the number.

B Listen. Circle the number you hear.

1. 0 (6) 16
2. 3 7 (20)
3. (1) 10 11
4. 2 5 15
5. 1 (9) 17
6. 11 (12) 20
7. (8) 9 10
8. 3 (5) 13
9. 14 15 (16)

C Listen. Write the number you hear.

1. _3_   3. _18_   5. _1_   7. _20_   9. _5_
2. _8_   4. _12_   6. _0_   8. _4_   10. _11_

D Write. Match the number and the word.

| 1 | 2 | 3 | 4 | 5 | 6 | 7 | 8 | 9 | 10 |

| three | five | four | two | one | nine | six | ten | eight | seven |

Talk with a partner. Take turns. Spell a number. Your partner says the number.

n-i-n-e

9

4 Days and months

A Listen and repeat.

STUDENT TK 8
CLASS CD1 TK 8

Sunday	Monday	Tuesday	Wednesday	Thursday	Friday	Saturday

Talk with a partner. Take turns. Say a day. Your partner points to the day.

B Write the full spelling.

1. Sun. ___Sunday___
2. Mon. _____
3. Tues. _____
4. Wed. _____

5. Thurs. _____
6. Fri. _____
7. Sat. _____

C Listen and repeat.

STUDENT TK 9
CLASS CD1 TK 9

1. January
2. February
3. March
4. April

5. May
6. June
7. July
8. August

9. September
10. October
11. November
12. December

Talk with a partner. Say a number. Your partner says the month.

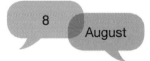

8
August

D Talk with a partner about your birthday. Take turns.

What month is your birthday?

June.

LESSON A
Listening

1 **Before you listen**

A Look at the picture. What do you see?

B Point to: first name • last name • city
zip code • area code • telephone number

REGISTRATION OFFICE

REGISTRATION HOURS
6 p.m. – 9 p.m.

COURSE SCHEDULE

SUBJECT	TEACHER'S NAME	ROOM NUMBER

LAST NAMES A-G

LAST NAMES H-P

LAST NAMES Q-Z

September

COURSE GUIDE

MR. CLARK

REGISTRATION FORM

Name	Svetlana Kulik
Phone	(707) 555-9073
Address	1041 Main Street Napa, California 94558

Unit Goals **Recognize** names and vocabulary for personal identification
Make introductions
Complete a registration form

UNIT 1

2 Listen

A Listen. Write the letter of the conversation.

STUDENT TK 10
CLASS CD1 TK 10

1. _C_

2. _E_

3. _B_

4. _F_

5. _D_

6. _a_

B Listen again to the conversations. Write the names and numbers you hear.

STUDENT TK 10
CLASS CD1 TK 10

A. _____555-8907_____

B. _____213_____ (Area Code)

C. _____MR. CLARK_____

D. _____1041 Main street_____

E. _____RICARDO_____

F. _____94558_____

Listen again. Check your answers.

3 After you listen

Write. Complete the sentences about yourself.

1. My first name is _Donghyum_ .

2. My last name is _Kim_ .

3. My area code is _678_ .

4. My telephone number is _678-598-4105_

Talk with a partner. Talk about yourself.

My first name is Dahlia.

My first name is Yuri.

Saying telephone numbers
Stop at each number. Say *oh* for *zero*.

5	5	5	-	2	0	1	6
five	- five	- five		two	- oh	- one	- six

LESSON **B** What's your name?

1 **Grammar focus: possessive adjectives**

Questions			Answers	
What's	**your**	name?	**My**	name is Svetlana.
What's	**his**	name?	**His**	name is Steve.
What's	**her**	name?	**Her**	name is Mary.
What are	**their**	names?	**Their**	names are Ted and Rob.

What's = What is

Turn to page 142 for a complete grammar chart.

2 **Practice**

A **Write.** Complete the sentences.
Use *his*, *her*, or *their*.

1. **A** What's _____*his*_____ first name?
   B _____*His*_____ first name is Alfred.

2. **A** What's _____*her*_____ first name?
   B _____*Her*_____ first name is Sue.

3. **A** What's _____*his*_____ first name?
   B _____*His*_____ first name is Tom.

4. **A** What's _____*their*_____ last name?
   B _____*Their*_____ last name is Jones.

CLASS CD1 TK 11

Listen and repeat. Then practice with a partner.

B **Talk** with a partner. Look at the student directory.
Change the **bold** words and make conversations.

> **A** What's **his** telephone number?
> **B** **His** telephone number is **555-9314**.

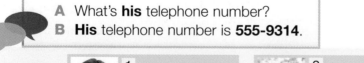

STUDENT DIRECTORY

1 555-9314	2 555-9847	3 555-2034
4 555-5093	5 555-6172	6 555-8216

C Listen. Then listen again and repeat.

CLASS CD1 TK 12

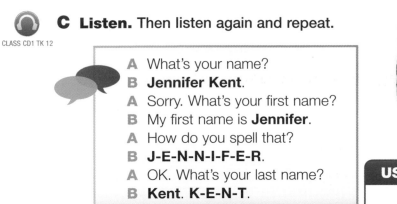

> A What's your name?
> B **Jennifer Kent**.
> A Sorry. What's your first name?
> B My first name is **Jennifer**.
> A How do you spell that?
> B **J-E-N-N-I-F-E-R**.
> A OK. What's your last name?
> B **Kent**. **K-E-N-T**.

USEFUL LANGUAGE

Please spell that.
How do you spell
Jennifer?

Talk in a group. Ask questions and write the names.

First name	Last name
Jennifer	Kent
Elafia	Abushama
Kang	Lee
Reyna	Lara

3 Communicate

A Talk with your classmates. Introduce a classmate.

> This is my classmate. Her first name is Jennifer. Her last name is Kent.

B Talk with a partner. Take turns and make new conversations.

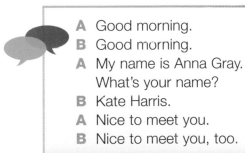

> A Good morning.
> B Good morning.
> A My name is Anna Gray. What's your name?
> B Kate Harris.
> A Nice to meet you.
> B Nice to meet you, too.

> A Hi. My name is Peter.
> B Hi. My name is Alan.
> A Nice to meet you, Alan.
> B Nice to meet you, too, Peter.

CULTURE NOTE

Some people have two first names: *Mei-hwa*.

Some people have two last names: *Baker-Price*.

☑ Use possessive adjectives (*my, your, his, her, their*) **UNIT 1 9**

LESSON C Are you from Canada?

1 Grammar focus: subject pronouns; simple present of *be*

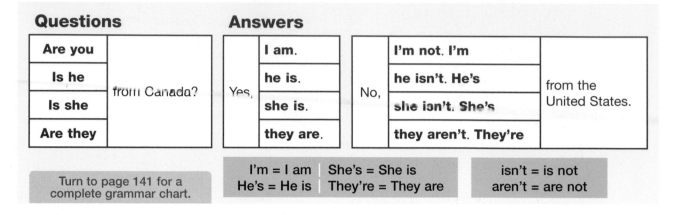

Questions		Answers			
Are you			I am.		
Is he	from Canada?	Yes,	he is.	No,	
Is she			she is.		from the United States.
Are they			they are.		

I'm not. I'm	
he isn't. He's	
she isn't. She's	
they aren't. They're	

Turn to page 141 for a complete grammar chart.

I'm = I am	She's = She is
He's = He is	They're = They are

isn't = is not
aren't = are not

2 Practice

A Write. Complete the sentences.

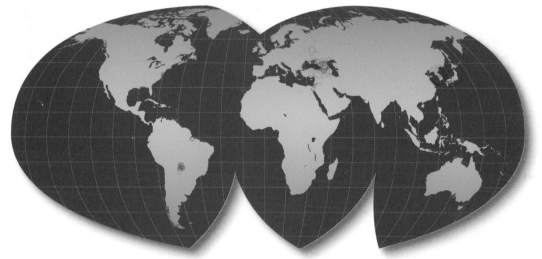

1. **A** _____Are_____ you from Canada?
   B No, I _'m not_____ .

2. **A** _____Are_____ they from Somalia?
   B Yes, _they are_____ .

3. **A** _____Is_____ she from Russia?
   B Yes, _she is_____ .

4. **A** _____Is_____ he from Mexico?
   B Yes, _he is_____ .

5. **A** _____Is_____ she from China?
   B No, _she isn't_____ .

6. **A** _____Are_____ they from Brazil?
   B No, _they aren't_____ .

7. **A** _____Is_____ he from Ecuador?
   B No, _he isn't_____ .

8. **A** _____Are_____ you from South Korea?
   B Yes, _I am_____ .

Listen and repeat. Then practice with a partner.

B **Talk** with a partner. Change the **bold** words and make conversations.

INTERNATIONAL FESTIVAL

A **Is he** from **Mexico**?
B Yes, **he is**.

A **Are they** from **the United States**?
B No, **they aren't**. **They're** from **India**.

1. Japan?   2. the United States?   3. Mexico?   4. India?   5. Mexico?   6. Japan?

C Listen and repeat. Then practice with a partner.

CLASS CD1 TK 14

A Where are you from, **Katia**?
B I'm from **Brazil**.
A **Brazil**? How do you spell that?
B **B-R-A-Z-I-L**.

> **USEFUL** LANGUAGE
>
> *Where are you from?*
> *Where do you come from?*
> *What country are you from?*

3 Communicate

Talk in a group. Where are your classmates from? Make guesses.

A This is Katia. Where is she from?
B Is she from Colombia?
A No, she isn't.
B Is she from Brazil?
A Yes, she is.

☑ Use subject pronouns (*I*, *you*, *he*, *she*, *they*); use *be* in the simple present   **UNIT 1**   11

LESSON D Reading

1 Before you read

Talk. Svetlana starts school today. Look at the registration form. Answer the questions.

1. What's her last name?
2. What's her telephone number?

REGISTRATION FORM

Name	Svetlana Kulik
Phone	(707) 555-9073
Address	1041 Main Street Napa, California 94558

2 Read

Listen and read.

STUDENT TK 11
CLASS CD1 TK 15

A New Student

Svetlana Kulik is a new student. She is from Russia. Now she lives in Napa, California. Her address is 1041 Main Street. Her zip code is 94558. Her area code is 707. Her telephone number is 555-9073.

Address with 3 numbers
832 Main Street
eight thirty-two
Address with 4 numbers
1041 Main Street
ten forty-one

3 After you read

A Read the sentences. Are they correct? Circle *Yes* or *No*.

1. Svetlana is a new teacher.   Yes   (No)
2. Her last name is Kulik.   (Yes)   No
3. She is from Colombia.   Yes   No
4. Her address is 1014 Main Street.   Yes   (No)
5. Her zip code is 94558.   (Yes)   No
6. Her area code is 555-9073.   Yes   (No)

Write. Correct the sentences.

1. Svetlana is a new <u>student</u>.

B Write. Answer the questions about Svetlana.

1. What is her last name? _Her last name is Kulik_
2. Is she from Russia? _Yes she is_
3. What is her address? _Her address is 1014 Main Street_
4. What is her telephone number? _Her telephone number is 555 - 9073_

4 **Picture dictionary** Personal information

Student ID

Mr. Rafael A. Gomez
263 Midlane Street, Apt. 3B
New York, NY 10012

Rafael A. Gomez

1. _____title_____

2. __address__

3. ___city___

4. __state__

5. _Signature_

9. _middle initial_

8. __street__

7. _apartment number_

6. _zip code_

A Write the words in the picture dictionary. Then listen and repeat.

STUDENT TK 12
CLASS CD1 TK 16

address	middle initial	street
apartment number	signature	title
city	state	zip code

B Talk with a partner. Use the words in 4A to ask questions. Complete the student ID with your partner's information.

> **CULTURE NOTE**
>
> Use *Mr.* for a man.
>
> Use *Ms.* for a woman.
>
> Use *Mrs.* for a married woman.
>
> Use *Miss* for an unmarried woman.

STUDENT ID

Donghyun Kim
11708 Tumbre ct
Fairfax VA 22030

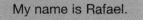

What's your name?

My name is Rafael.

LESSON E Writing

1 Before you write

A Talk with your classmates. Ask questions. Write the answers.

> A What's your name?
> B My name is **Liliana Lopez**.
> A What's your telephone number?
> B My telephone number is **555-2904**.
> A Where are you from?
> B I'm from **Mexico**.

> Begin names of people, streets, cities, states, and countries with capital letters.
> These are capital letters: *A B C D E . . . .*
> These are lowercase letters: *a b c d e . . . .*

Name	Telephone (phone) number	Country
Liliana Lopez	555-2904	Mexico
Blanca	703-991-9387	El-Salvador
Jaewoo Yoom	703-489-7233	Korea.
Kataya.	571-8399196	Bolivia.
Rosa.	703-832-2774	peru
Florencia	703-6498433	Ivory Cost
Reyna	571-314-7583	Homduras

B Write. Complete the sentences. Use the words in the box.

> address   last name   zip code
> area code   telephone number

Svetlana is a new student.

1. Her _____*last name*_____ is Kulik. She is from Russia.
2. Her _____ is 1041 Main Street.
3. Her _____ is 94558.
4. Her _____ is 555-9073.
5. Her _____ is 707.

C Write. Add capital letters.

STUDENT NEWS

P
~~p~~edro is a new student. He is single. He is from colombia. His last name is ramirez. His address is 285 pacheco street, houston, texas. His zip code is 77057. His telephone number is 555-7878. His area code is 713.

D Read about Pedro again. Complete the chart. Use capital letters.

First name	Last name	City	State
Pedro	Ramirez	Houston	Texas

2 Write

Read the questions and write about yourself.

> Begin sentences with capital letters.

1. What's your first name? _My first name is Donghyun_.
2. What's your last name? _Kim_.
3. What's your address? _11703 Tumbrel Ct Fairfax VA_.
4. What's your zip code? _2033_.
5. What's your phone number? _678-896-4403_.
6. Where are you from? _I am from Korea_.

3 After you write

A Read your sentences to a partner.

B Check your partner's sentences.

- What is your partner's name?
- Are the capital letters correct?

LESSON F Another view

1 Life-skills reading

REGISTRATION

Please print:

☒ Mr. ☐ Ms. ☐ Mrs.

(1) NAME: _____
     Last   First   Middle

(2) ADDRESS: _____
     Number   Street   Apt.

(3) _____
     City   State   Zip code

(4) TELEPHONE: _____
     Area code   Number

(5) COUNTRY OF ORIGIN: _____

(6) _____
                        Signature

A Read the questions. Look at the registration form. Fill in the answer.

1. Where do you print your country of origin?
   - Ⓐ line 1
   - Ⓑ line 2
   - ● line 5
   - Ⓓ line 6

2. Where do you print your name?
   - Ⓐ line 1
   - Ⓑ line 3
   - Ⓒ line 5
   - Ⓓ line 6

3. Where do you sign your name?
   - Ⓐ line 1
   - Ⓑ line 3
   - Ⓒ line 5
   - Ⓓ line 6

4. Where do you write your zip code?
   - Ⓐ line 2
   - Ⓑ line 3
   - Ⓒ line 4
   - Ⓓ line 5

B Write. Complete the form with your own information.

C Talk in a group. Look at your forms. Ask and answer questions.

What's your last name?

My last name is Hom.

2 Grammar connections: subject pronouns and possessive adjectives

Subject pronouns	Possessive adjectives	
I'm from Guatemala.	**My** name is Isabel.	**Contractions** I'm = I am you're = you are he's = he is she's = she is they're = they are
You're from Peru.	**Your** name is Leo.	
He's from Thailand.	**His** name is Dusit.	
She's from Iraq.	**Her** name is Amira.	
They're from South Korea.	**Their** last name is Kim.	

A **Talk** with a partner. Look at the picture. Take turns.

A *His* name is Victor.

B *He's* from Poland.

B **Work** in a group. Play the name game. Take turns.

3 Wrap up

Complete the **Self-assessment** on page 136.

☑ Scan and complete a registration form; contrast subject pronouns and possessive adjectives **UNIT 1** 17

LESSON **A**
Listening

1 **Before you listen**

A Look at the picture. What do you see?

B Point to: a book • a desk • a map • a pencil
a clock • an eraser • a pen • a table

LESSON
Review: name, address, phone number
New: school vocabulary
Book: Ventures, pages 18–29

Ava

Carmen

Franz

Mr. Liang

DICTIONARY

Unit Goals
Identify classroom objects
Identify location of classroom objects
Interpret information on a classroom inventory list

UNIT 2

2 Listen

A Listen. Write the letter of the conversation.

STUDENT TK 13
CLASS CD1 TK 17

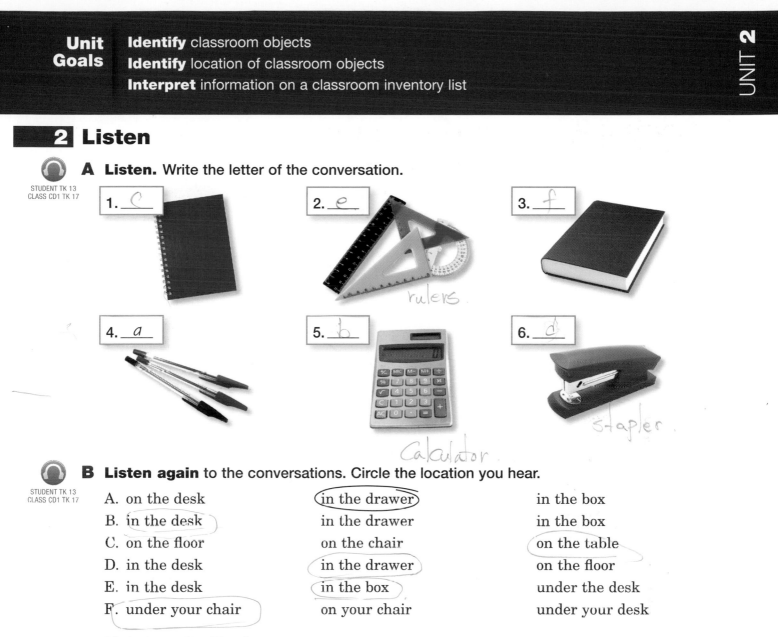

1. _C_

2. _e_   rulers

3. _f_

4. _a_

5. _b_   Calculator

6. _d_   stapler

B Listen again to the conversations. Circle the location you hear.

STUDENT TK 13
CLASS CD1 TK 17

A. on the desk | (in the drawer) | in the box
B. (in the desk) | in the drawer | in the box
C. on the floor | on the chair | (on the table)
D. in the desk | (in the drawer) | on the floor
E. in the desk | (in the box) | under the desk
F. (under your chair) | on your chair | under your desk

Listen again. Check your answers.

3 After you listen   * stuff

Write. What's on the desk? What's in the drawer? What's under the chair?

book   clock   paper   pencil   rulers   stapler

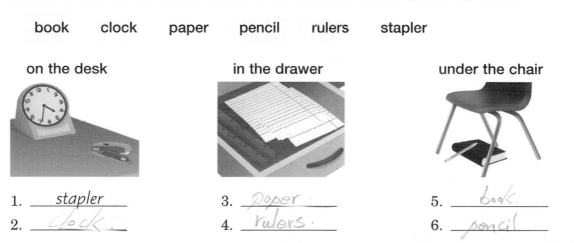

on the desk

1. ___stapler___
2. ___clock___

in the drawer

3. ___paper___
4. ___rulers___

under the chair

5. ___book___
6. ___pencil___

LESSON **B** Where is the pen?

1 Grammar focus: prepositions *in*, *on*, and *under*; *Where is?*

	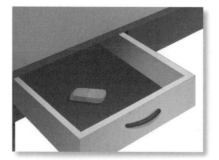		
Questions	Where's the pen?	Where's the pencil?	Where's the ruler?
Answers	It's **in** the drawer.	It's **on** the book.	It's **under** the notebook.

Where's = Where is

2 Practice

A Write. Complete the sentences. Use *in*, *on*, or *under*.

1. **A** Where's the book?
   B It's __on__ the shelf.

2. **A** Where's the pencil sharpener?
   B It's __on__ the wall.

3. **A** Where's the dictionary?
   B It's _under_ the table.

4. **A** Where's the calendar?
   B It's _under_ the box.

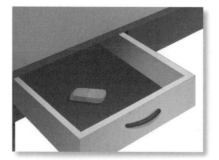

5. **A** Where's the eraser?
   B It's __in__ the drawer.

6. **A** Where's the calculator?
   B It's __in__ the cabinet.

Listen and repeat. Then practice with a partner.

CLASS CD1 TK 18

CLASS CD1 TK 19

B Listen. Circle the items you hear.

Talk with a partner. Look at the picture again. Change the **bold** words
and make conversations.

A Excuse me. Where's the **calculator**?
B It's **in the cabinet.**
A Oh, thanks.
B You're welcome.

USEFUL LANGUAGE

Say *excuse me* to get
someone's attention.

3 Communicate

Talk with a partner about your classroom.

Where's the computer?
It's on the table.

☑ Use prepositions (*in*, *on*, and *under*) to identify location; ask and answer *where* questions   UNIT 2   **21**

LESSON **C** Where are the pencils?

1 Grammar focus: singular and plural nouns

Singular

pencil   clock   book

Plural

more than

pencil**s**   clock**s**   book**s**

Questions

Is	the **pencil**	on the table?
Are	the **pencils**	

	is	the **pencil**?
Where	are	the **pencils**?

Answers

		it is.		it isn't.
Yes,			No,	
		they are.		they aren't.

It's		
	under the table.	
They're		

2 Practice

A Write. Look at the picture. Complete the conversations.

1. **A** Are the ____books____ in the cabinet?
   (book / books)
   B Yes, ____they are____ .

2. **A** Is the _____ under the clock?
   (calendar / calendars)
   B Yes, ____it is____ .

3. **A** Are the _____ on the table?
   (ruler / rulers)
   B No, ____they aren't____ .

4. **A** Are the _____ on the table?
   (pencil / pencils)
   B No, ____they aren't____ .

5. **A** Are the _____ on the table?
   (calculator / calculators)
   B Yes, ____they are____ .

Listen and repeat. Then practice with a partner.

10/6. ① Bruce.

B **Write.** Complete the sentences. Use *is* or *are*.

1. Where ___is___ the laptop computer?
2. Where ___are___ the notebooks?
3. Where ___is___ the calendar?

4. Where ___are___ the maps?
5. Where ___are___ the pencils?
6. Where ___is___ the calculator?

C **Write.** Look at the picture. Read the answers. Write the questions.

1. A *Where are the notebooks?*
   B They're in the filing cabinet.
2. A Where is the calculator?
   B It's on the filing cabinet.
3. A where is Calender ?
   B It's on the wall.

4. A Where is the laptop?
   B It's on the desk.
5. A where are the pencils?
   B They're under the dictionary.
6. A wher are the books ?
   B They're in the box.

Listen and repeat. Then practice with a partner.

CLASS CD1 TK 21

3 **Communicate**

Talk with a partner about things in your classroom.

> A Is the map on the desk?
> B Yes, it is.
> A Are the books on the table?
> B No, they aren't.
> A Where are they?
> B They're in the cabinet.

☑ Use singular and plural nouns; ask and answer *yes / no* and *where* questions   **UNIT 2** **23**

LESSON D Reading

1 Before you read

Talk. It's the first day of class. Look at the picture. Answer the questions.

1. What do you see in the classroom?
2. Where are the things?

2 Read

 Listen and read.

STUDENT TK 14
CLASS CD1 TK 22

Attention, new students!
Welcome to your new classroom.

- The laptop is on the small table.
- The pencils are in the basket on the desk.
- The erasers are in the basket.
- The books are in the bookcase.
- The calculators are in a box under the table.
- The markers are in the desk drawer.

> Look at pictures before you read. They help you understand new words. *Basket* is a new word. Find the basket in the picture.

3 After you read

A Read the sentences. Are they correct? Circle *Yes* or *No*.

1. The laptop is on the desk.	Yes	(No)
2. The pencils are under the table.	Yes	No
3. The erasers are in the bookcase.	Yes	No
4. The books are in the bookcase.	Yes	No
5. The calculators are under the table.	Yes	No
6. The markers are in the desk drawer.	Yes	No

Write. Correct the sentences.

1. The laptop is on the <u>small table</u>.

B Write. Answer the questions about the classroom.

1. Where is the box? _____

2. Where is the basket? _____

4 Picture dictionary Classroom objects

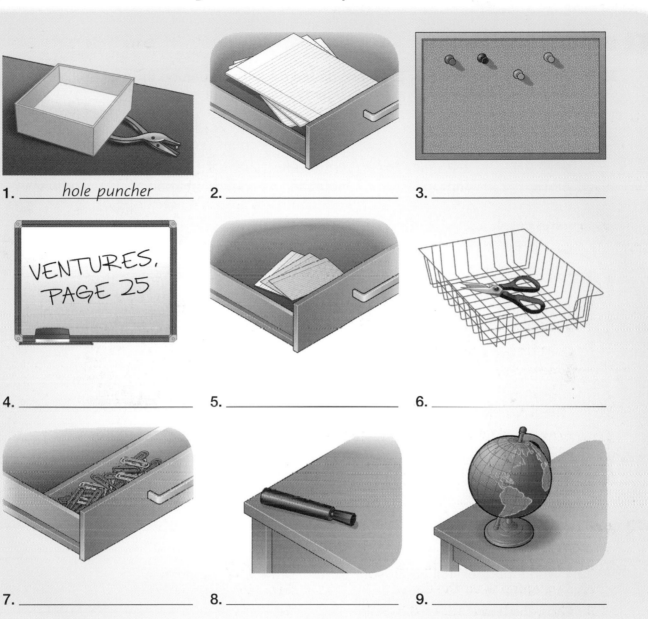

1. _____hole puncher_____

2. _____

3. _____

4. _____

5. _____

6. _____

7. _____

8. _____

9. _____

(whiteboard shows: VENTURES, PAGE 25)

A **Write** the words in the picture dictionary. Then listen and repeat.

STUDENT TK 15
CLASS CD1 TK 23

bulletin board	hole puncher	marker	paper clips	whiteboard
globe	index cards	notepads	scissors	

B **Talk** with a partner. Look at the pictures and make conversations.

A Where's the **whiteboard**?
B It's **on the wall**.
A Where are the **paper clips**?
B They're **in the drawer**.

☑ Read a notice about students' classroom; use vocabulary for classroom objects   **UNIT 2**   **25**

LESSON **E** Writing

1 Before you write

A **Draw.** Choose six objects. Draw two on the desk. Draw one on the wall. Draw two in the cabinet. Draw one under the table. Write the words under the picture.

calculator	dictionary	map	pen	ruler
calendar	hole puncher	notebook	pencil	scissors
clock	laptop	notepad	pencil sharpener	whiteboard

_____   _____   _____

_____   _____   _____

Talk with a partner. Tell about your picture. Draw your partner's objects here.

B Write. Look at the picture. Complete the sentences. Use *is* or *are* with *on*, *in*, or *under*.

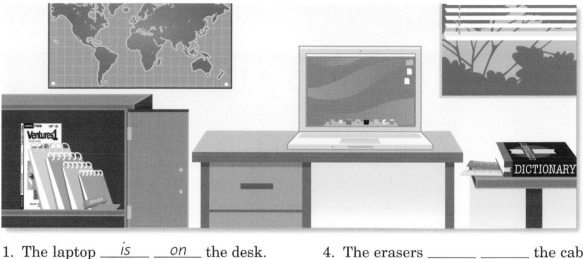

1. The laptop __is__ __on__ the desk.
2. The notepads _____ _____ the cabinet.
3. The book _____ _____ the cabinet.
4. The erasers _____ _____ the cabinet.
5. The map _____ _____ the wall.
6. The rulers _____ _____ the dictionary.

2 Write

A Write. Look at your classroom. What do you see? Complete the chart.

Singular	Plural
pen	pencils

B Write one sentence about each object.

1. *The pen is on the desk.*
2. *The pencils are in the drawer.*
3. _____
4. _____
5. _____
6. _____

> Start sentences with a capital letter (A, B, C). End sentences with a period (.).

3 After you write

A Read your sentences to a partner.

B Check your partner's sentences.

- What are four things in the classroom? Where are they?
- Are the capital letters and periods correct?

☑ Write sentences about the location of things in a classroom   **UNIT 2   27**

LESSON F Another view

1 Life-skills reading

Classroom Inventory List

Item		Number	Location
calculators		15	in the drawer
laptops		1	on the desk
books		15	under the table
erasers		20	in the box
pencils		20	on the table
pens		20	on the table
notebooks		25	under the table

A Read the questions. Look at the inventory list. Fill in the answer.

1. How many pencils are on the table?
   - (A) 5
   - (B) 15
   - (C) 20
   - (D) 25

2. What's on the desk?
   - (A) a pen
   - (B) a book
   - (C) a calculator
   - (D) a laptop

3. Where are the calculators?
   - (A) in the cabinet
   - (B) in the drawer
   - (C) on the desk
   - (D) under the table

4. Where are the books?
   - (A) under the table
   - (B) on the table
   - (C) on the desk
   - (D) in the box

B Talk with a partner. Ask and answer questions about the inventory list.

Are the pens on the table?

Yes, they are.

Where are the erasers?

They're in the box.

2 Grammar connections: *this / that* and *these / those*

This is a book.	**That's** a book.	that's = that is
These are books.	**Those** are books.	

A **Work** in a group. Put one or more objects in a bag. (Other classmates close their eyes.) Then take turns. Take an object from the bag. Ask questions.

Hector, are these your keys?

No, those aren't my keys.

Fen, are these your keys?

Yes, those are my keys.

B **Talk** with your group. Say what your object is. Get your object.

A *That's* my pencil.

B Here you are.

3 Wrap up

Complete the **Self-assessment** on page 136.

Review

1 Listening

Read the questions. Then listen and circle the answers.

1. What is Juan's last name?
   a. Perez *(circled)*
   b. Cruz

2. Where is he from?
   a. Mexico
   b. El Salvador

3. What is his apartment number?
   a. 1324
   b. 10

4. What is his zip code?
   a. 94548
   b. 94321

5. What is his area code?
   a. 213
   b. 555

6. What is his telephone number?
   a. 555-6301
   b. 555-0133

Talk with a partner. Ask and answer the questions. Use complete sentences.

2 Grammar

A Write. Complete the story.

A New Student

Layla _____is_____ a new student. _____Her_____ last name
     1. is / are   2. My / Her

is Azari. She _____is_____ from Iran. She _____is_____ a good
     3. is / are   4. is / are

student. Her pencils and a notebook _____are_____ on her
            5. is / are

desk. A dictionary is _____in_____ her bag. Her classmates
            6. in / at

_____aren't_____ in the classroom now.
7. isn't / aren't

B Write. Unscramble the words. Make questions about the story.

1. from / Where / Layla / is / ? _____Where is Layla from?_____
2. her / What's / name / last / ? _____what's her last name?_____
3. good / she / a / student / Is / ? _____Is she a good student?_____
4. in / bag / What / is / her / ? _____What is in her bag?_____

Talk with a partner. Ask and answer the questions.

3 Pronunciation: syllables

CLASS CD1 TK 25

A Listen to the syllables in these words.

•
name

• •
address

• • •
apartment

CLASS CD1 TK 26

B Listen and repeat. Say the word and clap one time for each syllable.

•	• •	• • •
map	classroom	telephone
books	middle	initial
box	partner	signature
clock	whiteboard	computer
pens	ruler	sharpener
chair	notebook	calendar
desk	pencil	eraser

Talk with a partner. Take turns. Say a word. Your partner claps for each syllable.

CLASS CD1 TK 27

C Listen to the words. Write the number of syllables you hear.

a. _____1_____   b. _____2_____   c. _____2_____   d. _____1_____

e. _____4_____   f. _____3_____   g. _____1_____   h. _____2_____

Listen again and repeat. Clap one time for each syllable.

D Write. Find ten other words in your book. Make a list.

1.	6.
2.	7.
3.	8.
4.	9.
5.	10.

Talk with a partner. Say the words. Your partner says the number of syllables.

UNIT 3 Friends and family

LESSON A
Listening

who lives with you?
I lives with

1 Before you listen

A Look at the picture. What do you see?

B Point to: the mother • the father • the daughter
the son • the grandmother • the grandfather

Unit Goals	**Identify** family members
	Identify family activities
	Complete a census form

UNIT 3

2 Listen

STUDENT TK 16
CLASS CD1 TK 28

A Listen. Write the letter of the conversation.

my name is Jean → Teacher.
× step son . step - daughter.
× step - grand son

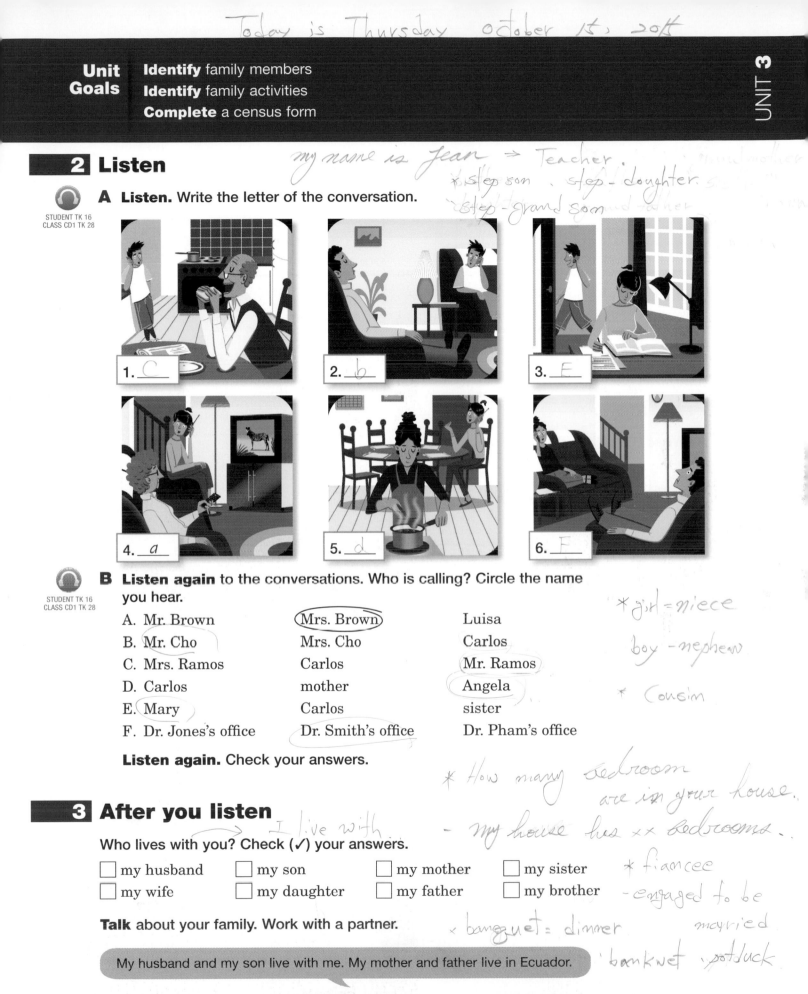

1. C

2. b

3. E

4. a

5. d

6. E

STUDENT TK 16
CLASS CD1 TK 28

B Listen again to the conversations. Who is calling? Circle the name you hear.

A. Mr. Brown	(Mrs. Brown)	Luisa
B. (Mr. Cho)	Mrs. Cho	Carlos
C. Mrs. Ramos	Carlos	(Mr. Ramos)
D. Carlos	mother	(Angela)
E. (Mary)	Carlos	sister
F. Dr. Jones's office	(Dr. Smith's office)	Dr. Pham's office

× girl = niece
boy - nephew
× Cousin

Listen again. Check your answers.

× How many bedroom are in your house.
- my house has ×× bedrooms.

3 After you listen

I live with

Who lives with you? Check (✓) your answers.

- ☐ my husband
- ☐ my wife
- ☐ my son
- ☐ my daughter
- ☐ my mother
- ☐ my father
- ☐ my sister
- ☐ my brother

× fiancee
- engaged to be married
× banquet = dinner
· bankwet , potluck

Talk about your family. Work with a partner.

> My husband and my son live with me. My mother and father live in Ecuador.

☑ Listen for and identify family activities and people's names **UNIT 3 33**

p 142.

LESSON B What are you doing?

p 142.

1 Grammar focus: present continuous; *What* questions

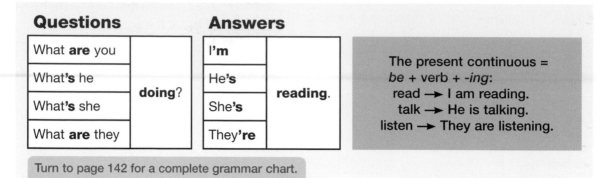

Questions			Answers		
What **are** you			I**'m**		
What**'s** he	**doing**?		He**'s**	**reading**.	
What**'s** she			She**'s**		
What **are** they			They**'re**		

The present continuous =
be + verb + *-ing*:
read → I am reading.
talk → He is talking.
listen → They are listening.

Turn to page 142 for a complete grammar chart.

2 Practice

A **Write.** Complete the conversations.

1. **A** What's she doing?
   B *She's reading.*
   (read)

2. **A** What's he doing?
   B *He's sleeping* .
   (sleep)

3. **A** What are they doing?
   B *They're eating* .
   (eat)

4. **A** What's he doing?
   B *he's watching* TV.
   (watch)

5. **A** What's she doing?
   B *She's talking* .
   (talk)

6. **A** What are you doing?
   B *They're studing* .
   (study)

Listen and repeat. Then practice with a partner.

CLASS CD1 TK 29

B **Talk** with a partner. Point to the picture. Change the **bold** words and make conversations.

| A | What's **she** doing? | | A | What are **they** doing? |
| | B | **She's listening to music.** | | B | **They're eating popcorn.** |

C **Write.** Answer the question.

What are you doing?

I'm _____.

Communicate

Talk. Practice with a partner.

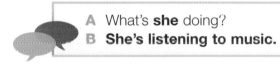

A	Hello?
B	Hi, Ann. This is Paul.
A	Oh, hi, Paul.
B	What are you doing?
A	I'm cooking dinner.
B	Oh, sorry. I'll call back later.

Make new conversations.

☑ Ask and answer *what* questions in the present continuous   **UNIT 3**   **35**

LESSON C Are you working now?

1 Grammar focus: present continuous; *Yes / No* questions

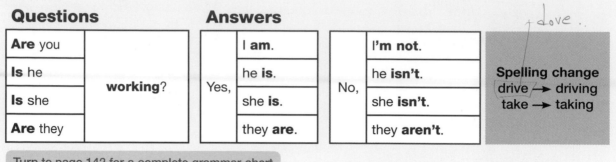

Questions		Answers				
Are you		Yes,	I **am**.	No,	I'**m not**.	*↑dove..*
Is he	**working**?		he **is**.		he **isn't**.	**Spelling change**
Is she			she **is**.		she **isn't**.	drive → driving
Are they			they **are**.		they **aren't**.	take → taking

Turn to page 142 for a complete grammar chart.

2 Practice

A Write. Complete the conversations.

1. **A** Is she ___working___ now?
   (work)
   B Yes, she is. She's very busy.

2. **A** Is he ___driving___ to work?
   (drive)
   B Yes, he is. He's late.

3. **A** Are they ___eating___ lunch now?
   (eat)
   B Yes, they are. They're hungry.

4. **A** Is he ___helping___ his grandmother?
   (help)
   B Yes, he is. He's really helpful.

5. **A** Is she ___taking___ a break?
   (take)
   B Yes, she is. She's tired.

6. **A** Are they ___buying___ water?
   (buy)
   B Yes, they are. They're thirsty.

Listen and repeat. Then practice with a partner.

B Look at the picture. Check (✓) *Yes* or *No*.

	Yes	No
1. Is Joe driving to work?	☐	✔
2. Is Mike helping his father?	✔	☐
3. Is Lisa talking to her brother?	✔	☐
4. Is Karla eating lunch?	✔	☐
5. Is Jennifer working now?	☐	✔
6. Are Peter and Paul buying soda?	☐	✔

Talk with a partner. Ask and answer questions.

> Is Joe driving to work?

> No, he isn't. He's cooking lunch.

3 Communicate

Talk with a partner. Take turns. Act out and guess a word from the box.

busy	thirsty
hungry	tired

driving	studying
eating	working

> Are you tired?

> Yes, I am.

> Are you working?

> No, I'm not.

☑ Ask and answer *yes / no* questions in the present continuous   **UNIT 3**   **37**

LESSON D Reading

1 Before you read

Talk. Juan is celebrating his birthday.
Look at the picture. Answer the questions.

1. What are the people doing?
2. Do you celebrate birthdays? How?

Photo Album

2 Read

 Listen and read.

STUDENT TK 17
CLASS CD1 TK 31

The Birthday Party

My name is Juan. In this picture, it's my birthday. I am 70 years old. Look at me! I don't look 70 years old. My wife, my daughter, and my grandson are eating cake. My grandson is always hungry. My granddaughter is drinking soda. She's always thirsty. My son-in-law is playing the guitar and singing. Everyone is happy!

> Think about the title before you read. This helps you understand the story.

3 After you read

A Read the sentences. Are they correct? Circle *Yes* or *No*.

1. Juan is 17 years old.	Yes	(No)
2. Juan is celebrating his birthday with his ~~friends~~ *family*.	Yes	(No)
3. His wife, daughter, and grandson are eating cake.	(Yes)	No
4. His granddaughter is drinking soda.	(Yes)	No
5. His grandson is playing the guitar and singing.	Yes	(No)
6. Everyone is tired.	Yes	(No)

Write. Correct the sentences.

1. Juan is 70 years old.

B Write. Answer the questions about Juan's party.

1. What is the family celebrating? _Juan_
2. What is the family eating? _His wife, daughter and grandson_
3. What is Juan's granddaughter doing? _She is drinking soda_
4. What is his son-in-law doing? _His playing the guitar._

4 Picture dictionary Family members

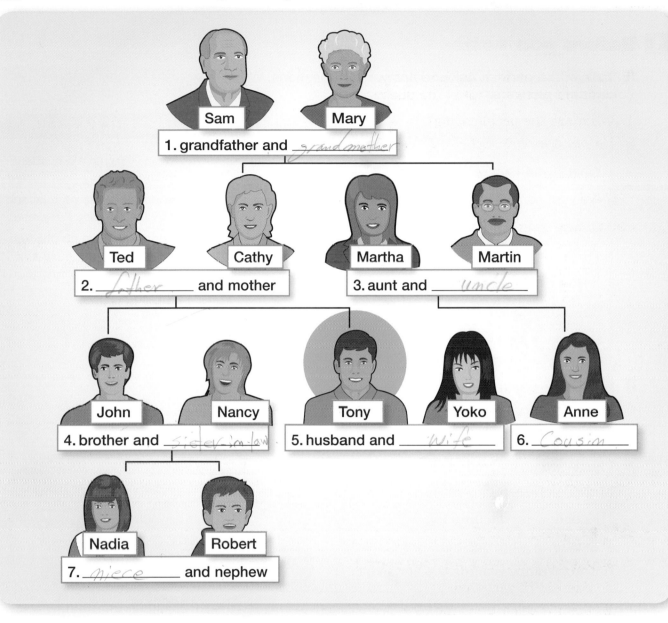

Sam   Mary

1. grandfather and _grandmother_

Ted   Cathy   Martha   Martin

2. _father_ and mother   3. aunt and _uncle_

John   Nancy   Tony   Yoko   Anne

4. brother and _sister-in-law_   5. husband and _wife_   6. _Cousin_

Nadia   Robert

7. _niece_ and nephew

STUDENT TK 18
CLASS CD1 TK 32

A Write. Look at Tony. Complete his family tree. Then listen and repeat.

cousin   grandmother   sister-in-law   wife
father   niece   uncle

B Talk with a partner. Take turns. Ask and answer questions about Tony's family.

Who is Yoko?

She's Tony's wife.

USEFUL LANGUAGE

Dad = father
Mom = mother
Grandpa = grandfather
Grandma = grandmother
Tony's wife = wife of Tony

☑ Read a paragraph about a family birthday party; use vocabulary for family members   **UNIT 3   39**

LESSON E Writing

1 Before you write

A **Talk** with a partner. Ask and answer the questions. Write your partner's answers.

U.S. Census Bureau

What's your name?	
Are you married or single?	
Do you have children?	
How many daughters?	
How many sons?	
How many sisters do you have?	
How many brothers do you have?	

USEFUL LANGUAGE

When you have a husband or wife, you say *I'm married.*

When you have no husband or wife, you say *I'm single.*

When you have no children, you say *I don't have any.*

B **Read.** Then write the words on the picture.

My name is David. I am single.

I live with my sister and her husband.

I have two nieces and one nephew.

In this picture, my nieces are <u>cooking</u>.

My nephew is <u>watching</u> TV.

My sister is <u>studying</u>. She's very smart.

Her husband is <u>reading</u> the newspaper.

2. _____

3. _____

4. _____

1. ____*cooking*____

2 Write

A Draw your family. What are they doing?

B Write. Answer the questions.

Spell numbers from one to ten:
*I have **one** brother*.
Write all other numbers: *I have **11** nieces*.

1. What's your name?

   My name is ___Donghyun Kim___.

2. Are you married or single?

   I'm ___married___.

3. Who do you live with?

   I live with ___my wife and two daughter and one son___.

4. How many are in your family?

   I have ___five people in my family___.

5. In the picture, what are they doing?

   ___My wife is computer working and old daughter is studing___
   ___and another daughter and son watchig TV___

3 After you write

A Read your sentences to a partner.

B Check your partner's sentences.

* How many people are in the family?
* Did your partner spell the numbers from one to ten?

LESSON F Another view

1 Life-skills reading

Insurance Application Form				
Last name	**First name**	**Age**	**Male**	**Female**
Parents				
Clark	Joseph	30	x	
Clark	Rita	29		x
Children				
Clark	Justin	10	x	
Clark	Scott	8	x	
Clark	Carolyn	7		x
Clark	Michael	2	x	

A Read the questions. Look at the form. Fill in the answer.

1. How many children do Mr. and Mrs. Clark have?
   - (A) 1
   - (B) 2
   - (C) 3
   - (D) 4 ✓

2. How many daughters do Mr. and Mrs. Clark have?
   - (A) 1 ✓
   - (B) 2
   - (C) 3
   - (D) 4

3. How many sons do Mr. and Mrs. Clark have?
   - (A) 1
   - (B) 2
   - (C) 3 ✓
   - (D) 4

4. Who is eight years old?
   - (A) Carolyn
   - (B) Justin
   - (C) Michael
   - (D) Scott ✓

B Talk in a group. Ask and answer questions about the Clark family.

How old is Michael?

He's two years old.

2 Grammar connections: object pronouns

Object pronouns		
I like <u>Johnny Depp</u>.	I like **him**.	I don't know him. I don't know her.
I don't like <u>Shakira</u>.	I don't like **her**.	
Katia likes <u>chocolate</u>.	She likes **it**.	
Peter likes <u>cats</u>.	He likes **them**.	

A Talk with your classmates. Complete the chart.

A Do you like chocolate, Peter?

B No, I don't. I don't like *it*.

A Do you like chocolate, Katia?

C Yes, I do. I like *it*.

Find someone who likes . . .	Name
chocolate	*Katia*
Johnny Depp	I like
dogs	
milk	
Shakira	I like it
Prince William and Princess Kate	
TV	
birthdays	I like them
Lionel Messi (soccer player)	
guitars	I like them

B Share your group's information with the class.

Katia likes chocolate. Peter doesn't like it.

3 Wrap up

Complete the **Self-assessment** on page 137.

LESSON A
Listening

1 Before you listen

A Look at the picture. What do you see?

B Point to a person with: a backache • a cough • a headache
a broken leg • an earache • a sore throat

Unit Goals
Identify common health problems
Identify remedies for common health problems
Write a note to excuse an absence

UNIT 4

2 Listen

STUDENT TK 19
CLASS CD1 TK 33

A Listen. Write the letter of the conversation.

1. _____

2. _a_

3. _____

4. _____

5. _____

6. _____

STUDENT TK 19
CLASS CD1 TK 33

B Listen again to the conversations. Circle the words you hear.

A. I'm sorry to hear it. (I'm sorry to hear that.) I'm sorry about that.
B. I hope it gets better soon. I hope you get better soon. I hope you get well soon.
C. I hope it gets better soon. I hope you get better soon. I hope you get well soon.
D. That's too bad. That's terrible. I'm sorry.
E. That's too bad. Oh, I'm sorry. That's terrible.
F. That's too bad. Oh, that's terrible. I'm sorry.

Listen again. Check your answers.

3 After you listen

Talk with a partner. Take turns. Act out and guess the problem.

Sore throat?

Yes

USEFUL LANGUAGE

Yes.
That's right.
No. Guess again.

LESSON B I have a headache.

1 Grammar focus: simple present of *have*

Statements

I	**have**
You	**have**
He	**has**
She	**has**

a cold.

Turn to page 144 for a complete grammar chart.

Turn to page 144 for a complete grammar chart.

USEFUL LANGUAGE

*I have a **terrible** cold.*
*I have a **bad** headache.*

2 Practice

A Write. Complete the sentences. Use *has* or *have*.

1.

He __has__ a terrible cold.

2.

I __have__ a headache.

3.

He __has__ a backache.

4.

You __have__ a fever.

5.

I __have__ a broken arm.

6.
He __has__ a stomachache.

7.

She __has__ a bad cough.

8.

You __have__ a sore throat.

9.

She __has__ a cut.

Listen and repeat.

CLASS CD1 TK 34

Vote . Ballot

B **Talk** with a partner. Change the **bold** words and make conversations.

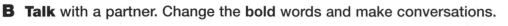

> A How **is she**?
> B Not so good.
> A What's wrong?
> B **She has a cold.**
> A I have **tissues**.
> B Really? Thanks.

USEFUL LANGUAGE

What's wrong?
What's the matter?

1.

she / a cold / tissues

2.

he / a headache / aspirin

3.

you / a cough / cough drops

4.

she / a cut / a bandage

5.

you / a sprained ankle / an ice pack

6.

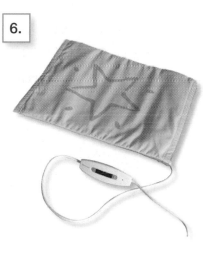

he / a backache / a heating pad

3 Communicate

Talk with a partner. Ask and answer questions.

> A What's the matter?
> B I have a cold.
> A Use tissues.

> A What's the matter?
> B I have a cough.
> A Take cough drops.

USEFUL LANGUAGE

Use: tissues, a bandage, a heating pad, an ice pack

Take: medicine, aspirin, vitamin C, cough drops

LESSON C Do you have a cold?

1 Grammar focus: questions with *have*

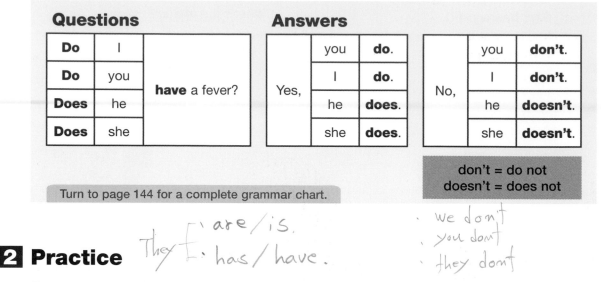

Questions		
Do	I	
Do	you	**have** a fever?
Does	he	
Does	she	

Answers						
Yes,	you	**do**.		No,	you	**don't**.
	I	**do**.			I	**don't**.
	he	**does**.			he	**doesn't**.
	she	**does**.			she	**doesn't**.

don't = do not
doesn't = does not

Turn to page 144 for a complete grammar chart.

2 Practice

(handwritten) They — are / is. has / have.

(handwritten) • we don't • you don't • they don't

A Write. Complete the sentences. Use *do*, *does*, *don't*, or *doesn't*.

1. Do I have a fever?
   No, you don't.

2. Does she have a sore throat?
   _____

3. Does he have a cough?
   Yes, he does

4. Do you have a cold?
   _____

5. Does she have the flu?
   _____

6. Does she have a sprained ankle?
   _____

Listen and repeat. Then practice with a partner.

CLASS CD1 TK 35

48 UNIT 4

B **Talk** with a partner. Change the **bold** words and make conversations.

> **A** **Mr. Jones** isn't at work today.
> **B** Why not? Does **he** have the flu?
> **A** No, not the flu. A **backache**.

USEFUL LANGUAGE

In conversational English, answers are often single words and short phrases rather than complete sentences.

Does he have the flu?

No, not the flu. = He doesn't have the flu.

1. Mr. Jones

a backache

2. Diana

a cold

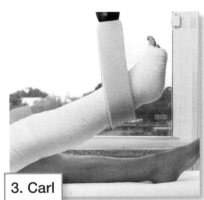

3. Carl

a broken leg

4. Mrs. Leeds

a stomachache

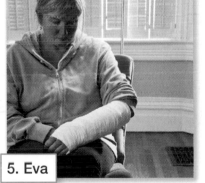

5. Eva

a broken arm

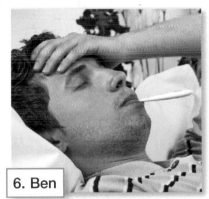

6. Ben

a fever

3 Communicate

Talk with a partner. Take turns and make conversations.

> **A** I don't feel well.
> **B** Do you have a cold?
> **A** No, I don't. I have a sore throat.
> **B** That's too bad. I hope you feel better.

USEFUL LANGUAGE

Get some rest.

I hope you feel better.

LESSON D Reading

1 Before you read

Talk. Maria is in the doctor's office. Look at the picture. Answer the questions.

1. Who is with Maria?
2. What's wrong?

2 Read

Listen and read.

STUDENT TK 20
CLASS CD1 TK 36

The Doctor's Office

Poor Maria! Everyone is sick! Maria and her children are in the doctor's office. Her son, Luis, has a sore throat. Her daughter, Rosa, has a stomachache. Her baby, Gabriel, has an earache. Maria doesn't have a sore throat. She doesn't have a stomachache. And she doesn't have an earache. But Maria has a very bad headache!

> Look at the exclamation points (!) in the reading. An exclamation point shows strong feeling.

· ch
= choose
= ache

3 After you read

A Read the sentences. Are they correct? Circle *Yes* or *No*.

1. Maria and her children are at school. Yes (No)   *in the doctor's office.*
2. Luis has a backache. *Sore throat* Yes No
3. Rosa has a headache. *stomachache.* Yes No
4. Gabriel has an earache. (Yes) No
5. Maria has a bad headache. (Yes) No
6. Everyone is happy today. Yes (No)   *They are unhappy.*
   sick
   not happy.

Write. Correct the sentences.

1. Maria and her children are <u>*in the doctor's office.*</u>

B Write. Answer the questions.

1. Does Maria have a cold? _____ *No she doesn't / She has a bad headache.*
2. Do Luis and Rosa have headaches? _____ *No. They doesn't / Luis has a earache*
3. What's the matter with Maria's children? _____ *and Rosa has a stomachache.*

4 **Picture dictionary** Parts of the body

- are
- have - possess.

Arabic 以 zh
large.

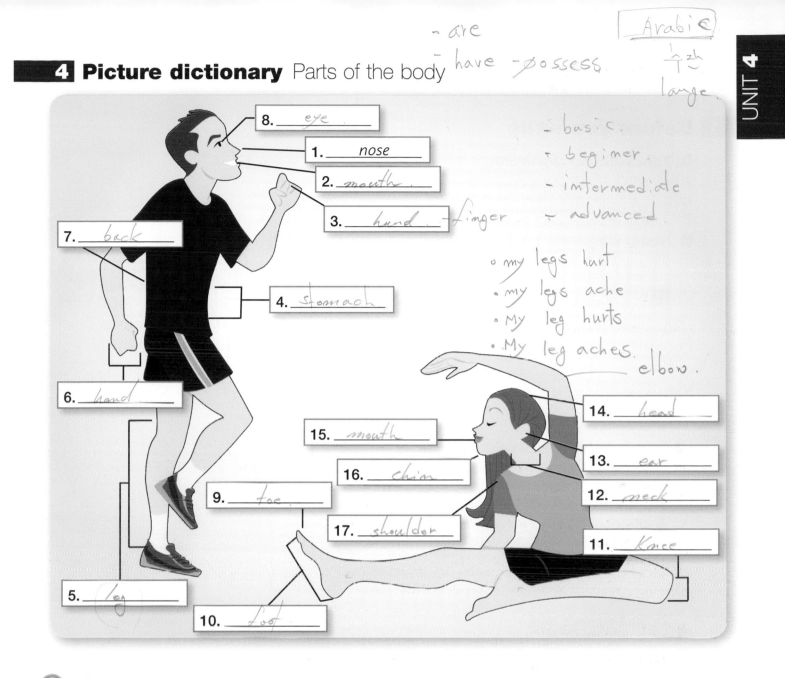

8. ___eye___

1. ___nose___

2. ___mouth___

3. ___hand___ *finger*

7. ___back___

- basic.
- beginner.
- intermediate
- advanced

4. ___Stomach___

○ my legs hurt
○ my legs ache
○ My leg hurts
○ My leg aches.
elbow.

6. ___hand___

15. ___mouth___

16. ___chin___

14. ___head___

13. ___ear___

12. ___neck___

9. ___toe___

17. ___shoulder___

11. ___Knee___

5. ___leg___

10. ___foot___

A **Write** the words in the picture dictionary. Then listen and repeat.

STUDENT TK 21
CLASS CD1 TK 37

| back | ear | finger | hand | knee | mouth | nose | stomach | toe |
| chin | eye | foot | head | leg | neck | shoulder | teeth |

B **Talk** with a partner. Change the **bold** word and make conversations.

A What's wrong?
B My **tooth** hurts.
A That's too bad.

one **tooth**
two **teeth**

☑ Read a paragraph about health problems; use vocabulary for parts of the body **UNIT 4** **51**

LESSON **E** Writing

1 Before you write

A **Talk** with your classmates.

1. Do you write notes?
2. Who do you write to?

B **Read.** Luis is sick today. Read the note from his mother to his teacher.

Maria Martinez	
	May 20, 2013

Write dates like this:

month	day	year
May	**20,**	**2013**
5 /	**20 /**	**13**

Dear Mrs. Jackson,

Luis Martinez is my son. He is at home today. He is sick. He has a sore throat. Please excuse him.

Thank you.

Sincerely,

Maria Martinez

Read the note again. Circle the information.

1. the date   *May 20, 2013*
2. the teacher's name   *Mrs. Jackson*
3. the name of the sick child   *Luis Martinez*
4. what's wrong   *He is sick. He has a sore throat.*
5. the signature   *Maria Martinez*

Write. Answer the questions.

1. What is the date? _____ *May 20, 2013* _____

2. What is the teacher's name? _____ *Mrs. Jackson* _____

3. Who is sick? _____ *Luis Martinez* _____

4. What's the matter? _____ *He has a sore throat.* _____

5. Who is the note from? _____ *Luis Martinez* _____

C **Write** about Rosa. She is sick, too. Complete the note.

| daughter | Dear | home | May 20, 2013 | stomachache |

May 20, 2013

Dear Mr. O'Hara,

Rosa Martinez is my _daughter_. She is at _home_ today. She is sick. She has a _stomachache_. Please excuse her.

Thank you.

Sincerely,
Maria Martinez

2 Write

Write. Imagine your son or daughter is sick today. Complete the note to the teacher.

May 20, 2013

Dear _Mrs. Jorge_,

(2) _Danial Kim_ is my _son_.
They are / He is at home today. _They are / He_ is sick.
They / He has a fever. Please excuse _him / them_.

Thank you.

Sincerely,
Donghyun Kim

3 After you write

A **Read** your note to a partner.

B **Check** your partner's note.

- Who is sick? What's the matter?
- Is the date correct?

LESSON F Another view

✚ Appointment Confirmation
Here is your appointment information.

Patient: _J. D. Avona_

Medical record number: _9999999_

Date: _Monday, October 23_

Time: _9:10 a.m._

Doctor: _William Goldman, MD_

Address: _Eye Care Clinic_

2025 Morse Avenue

Cancellation Information

To cancel only: (973) 555-5645   7 days / 24 hours

To cancel and reschedule: (973) 555-5210   Mon-Fri 8:30 a.m. to 5:00 p.m.

A **Read** the questions. Look at the appointment confirmation card.
Fill in the answer.

1. What is the doctor's last name?

   Ⓐ Avona

   Ⓑ Goldman

   Ⓒ Morse

   Ⓓ William

2. What is the appointment for?

   Ⓐ ears

   Ⓑ eyes

   Ⓒ nose

   Ⓓ throat

3. What is the address?

   Ⓐ Monday

   Ⓑ MD

   Ⓒ 2025 Morse Avenue

   Ⓓ 2025 Morris Avenue

4. What do you do to reschedule?

   Ⓐ call J. D. Avona

   Ⓑ call (973) 555-5645

   Ⓒ call (973) 555-5210

   Ⓓ go to the Eye Care Clinic

B **Talk** with your classmates. Ask and answer the questions.

1. Do you have a doctor?
2. Do you get appointment cards?
3. What information is on your appointment cards?

2 Grammar connections: *have* and *need*

have + problem	*need* + medicine / object
Do you **have** a headache?	Yes, I do. I **need** aspirin.
I **have** a headache.	You **need** aspirin.

A Talk with a partner. Look at the picture. Say what you need.
Your partner guesses what health problem you have. Take turns.

A I *need* a heating pad.

B Do you *have* a sprained ankle?

A No, I don't.

B Do you *have* a backache?

A Yes, I do!

B Tell the class about your partner's problems from 2A.

> Julia has a backache. She needs a heating pad.

3 Wrap up

Complete the **Self-assessment** on page 137.

☑ Scan for information on a medical appointment card; contrast *have* and *need*   **UNIT 4   55**

Review

CLASS CD1 TK 38

Read the questions. Then listen and circle the answers.

1. What's wrong with Connie?
   a. She has a backache.
   b. She has a headache.

2. What's wrong with Robert?
   a. He has an earache.
   b. He has a headache.

3. What's Robert doing?
   a. He's talking to the doctor.
   b. He's talking to the children.

4. What's Connie's daughter doing?
   a. She's sleeping.
   b. She's watching TV.

5. What's Connie's son doing?
   a. He's eating.
   b. He's watching TV.

6. What's wrong with Eddie?
   a. He has an earache.
   b. He has a stomachache.

Talk with a partner. Ask and answer the questions. Use complete sentences.

2 Grammar

A Write. Complete the story.

At the Hospital

This week, everyone in Anthony's family is sick. Anthony _____has_____
                                                          1. have / has
a wife, a son, and a daughter. Right now, they _____ sitting in
                                                    2. is / are
a hospital room. Anthony's wife _____ a backache. The nurse
                                    3. have / has
_____ giving her medicine. The doctor _____ talking to
  4. is / are   5. is / are
Anthony. He _____ asking questions about his children. They
              6. is / are
_____ the flu.
  7. have / has

B Write. Unscramble the words. Make questions about the story.

1. Is / home / family / at / Anthony's / ? _____*Is Anthony's family at home?*_____

2. is / doing / the nurse / What / ? _____

3. wrong / the children / with / What's / ? _____

Talk with a partner. Ask and answer the questions.

3 Pronunciation: strong syllables

A Listen to the syllables in these words.

CLASS CD1 TK 39

•
happy   •
            fever

B Listen and repeat. Clap for each syllable. Clap loudly for the strong syllable.

CLASS CD1 TK 40

•	• •	• • •	• • •
son	cooking	yesterday	tomorrow
wife	homework	grandmother	computer
head	toothache	grandfather	
ear	headache	newspaper	
foot	husband	studying	
leg	daughter	stomachache	

Talk with a partner. Take turns. Say a word. Your partner claps for each syllable.

C Listen for the strong syllable in each word. Put a dot (•) over the strong syllable.

CLASS CD1 TK 41

1. •
   father
2. earache
3. tired
4. birthday

5. thirsty
6. celebrate
7. finger
8. Brazil

9. repeat
10. elbow
11. reschedule
12. shoulder

D Write eight words from Units 3 and 4. Put a dot over the strong syllable in each word.

1.	5.
2.	6.
3.	7.
4.	8.

Talk with a partner. Read the words.

LESSON A
Listening

1 Before you listen

A Look at the picture. What do you see?

B Point to: a grocery store • a library • a restaurant
a hospital • a house • a street

Unit
Goals

Identify places around town
Identify locations of places
Write directions to a place

2 Listen

A Listen. Write the letter of the conversation.

STUDENT TK 22
CLASS CD1 TK 42

1. ____

2. ____

3. *a*

pharmacy   beauty

4. ____

5. ____

6. ____

B Listen again to the conversations. Circle the street you hear.

STUDENT TK 22
CLASS CD1 TK 42

A. 15th Avenue	(5th Avenue)	50th Avenue
B. C Street	G Street	Z Street
C. 7th Street	16th Street	70th Street
D. C Street	G Street	Z Street
E. Fir Avenue	First Avenue	Third Avenue
F. Thirteenth Avenue	Thirtieth Avenue	Third Avenue

Listen again. Check your answers.

3 After you listen

Write. How many places are in your neighborhood?

museums _____0_____	libraries _____	schools _____
pharmacies _____	restaurants _____	post offices _____
bus stops _____	parks _____	hospitals _____

Work with a partner. Ask and answer questions.

> How many museums are in your neighborhood?
>
> None.

USEFUL LANGUAGE

When *0* means *zero*,
say *none*.

☑ Listen for and identify places in the community   **UNIT 5   59**

LESSON **B** It's on the corner.

1 Grammar focus: *on, next to, across from, between, on the corner of*

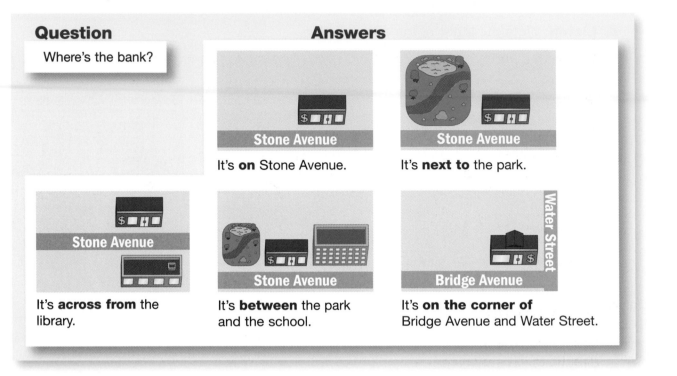

Question	Answers
Where's the bank?	It's **on** Stone Avenue.
	It's **next to** the park.
	It's **across from** the library.
	It's **between** the park and the school.
	It's **on the corner of** Bridge Avenue and Water Street.

2 Practice

A **Write.** Look at the map. Complete the sentences.

1. **A** Where's the park?
   B It's _____*next to*_____ the bank.

2. **A** Where's the library?
   B It's _____ the bank.

3. **A** Where's the school?
   B It's _____ First Street and Grant Avenue.

4. **A** Where's the hospital?
   B It's _____ Grant Avenue.

5. **A** Where's the bank?
   B It's _____ the school and the park.

6. **A** Where's the post office?
   B It's _____ the library.

Listen and repeat. Then practice with a partner.

CLASS CD1 TK 43

CLASS CD1 TK 44

B Listen and repeat.

> A Excuse me. **Where's Kim's Coffee Shop?**
> B It's **on Kent Street**.
> A Sorry. Could you repeat that, please?
> B It's **on Kent Street**.
> A Oh, OK. Thanks.

USEFUL LANGUAGE

Could you repeat that, please?
Sorry, I didn't get that.

Talk with a partner. Change the **bold** words and make conversations.

1. coffee shop   2. pharmacy   3. grocery store

Now practice this conversation with the map on page 60.

3 Communicate

A Talk with a partner. Look at the map on page 60. Take turns. Give directions. Guess the place.

> A It's on the corner of First Street and Grant Avenue. It's across from the hospital.
> B The school?
> A That's right.

B Draw these places on the map. Talk with a partner. Ask and answer questions about your maps.

bank
bus stop
coffee shop
grocery store
hospital
house

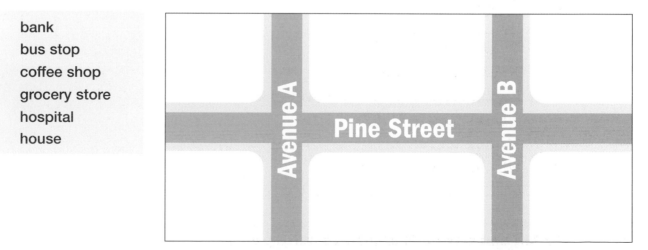

☑ Use prepositions to give the location of a place   **UNIT 5**   61

LESSON **C** Go two blocks.

1 Grammar focus: imperatives

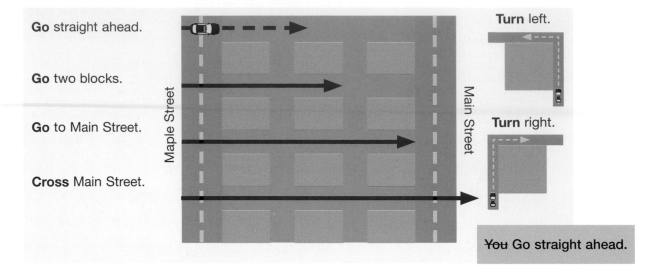

Go straight ahead.

Go two blocks.

Go to Main Street.

Cross Main Street.

Turn left.

Turn right.

~~You~~ Go straight ahead.

2 Practice

A Write. Match the pictures and the directions.

Cross Union Street.   Go three blocks.   Turn left.
Go straight ahead.   Go to Main Street.   Turn right.

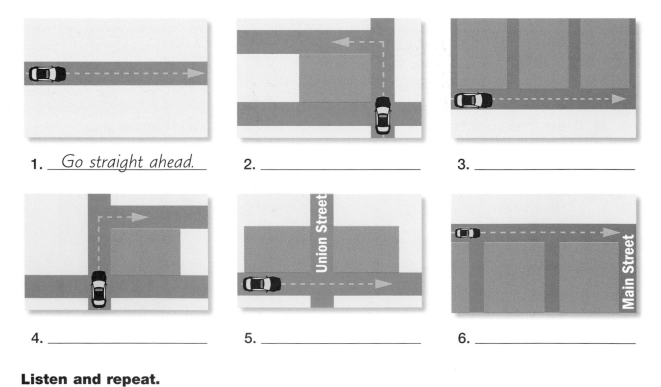

1. _Go straight ahead._   2. _____   3. _____

4. _____   5. _____   6. _____

🎧 **Listen and repeat.**

LESSON **D** Reading

1 Before you read

Talk. Look at these photos of Sandra's new neighborhood. Answer the questions.

1. What are the places in her neighborhood?
2. What can you do in these places?

2 Read

Listen and read.

STUDENT TK 23
CLASS CD1 TK 47

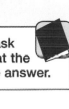

Hi Angela,

I love my new house. My neighborhood is great! Here are some pictures. There is a school on my street. My children go to the school. They like it a lot. There is a community center across from the school. My husband works at the community center. He walks to work. There is a grocery store next to my house. It's a small store, but we can buy a lot of things. There is a good Mexican restaurant on Second Street. It's right across from my house.

I like it here, but I miss you. Please write.

Your friend,

Sandra

When you see pronouns (*he*, *it*, *they*), ask *Who is the writer talking about?* Look at the sentences before a pronoun to find the answer.

3 After you read

A **Read** the sentences. Are they correct? Circle *Yes* or *No*.

1. Sandra lives on Summit Street.	Yes	(No)
2. There is a school on Sandra's street.	Yes	No
3. There is a community center next to the school.	Yes	No
4. Sandra's husband works at the community center.	Yes	No
5. Sandra's husband drives to work.	Yes	No

Write. Correct the sentences.

1. Sandra lives on <u>Second Street</u>.

B **Write.** Answer the questions about Sandra's neighborhood.

1. Where is the school? _____

2. Where is the grocery store? _____

3. Is the restaurant good? _____

B Read the directions. Look at the map. Write the places.

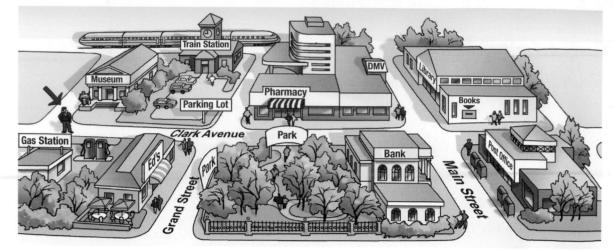

1. Go two blocks. Turn left. It's across from the library.   _the DMV_

2. Go straight. Cross Grand Street. Turn right
   on Main Street. It's across from the post office.   _____

3. Go to Grand Street. Turn left. It's next to the
   parking lot on Grand.   _____

4. Go one block. Turn right on Grand Street. It's
   across from Ed's Restaurant.   _____

Listen and repeat.

CLASS CD1 TK 46

C Talk with a partner. Look at the map in 2B. Change the **bold** words and
make conversations.

> **A** Excuse me. How do I get to the **DMV**?
> **B** **Go two blocks. Turn left.**
>   **It's on Main Street.**
> **A** OK. **Go two blocks. Turn left.**
>   **It's on Main Street.**
> **B** Right.
> **A** Thank you.

CULTURE NOTE

The DMV is the
Department of Motor
Vehicles. You can get a
driver's license there.

1. DMV	3. pharmacy	5. hospital
2. parking lot	4. library	6. post office

3 Communicate

Talk with a partner. Give directions to a building on the map in 2B. Your
partner names the building.

> Go two blocks. Turn left. It's on Main Street.
>> The DMV.

☑ Use imperatives (*Go, Cross, Turn*) to give directions   **UNIT 5   63**

4 Picture dictionary Places around town

1. _a shopping mall_

2. _____

3. _____

4. _____

5. _____

6. _____

7. _____

8. _____

9. _____

STUDENT TK 24
CLASS CD1 TK 48

A **Write** the words in the picture dictionary. Then listen and repeat.

an apartment building	a hardware store	a police station
a courthouse	a high school	a senior center
a day-care center	a playground	a shopping mall

B **Talk** with a partner about your neighborhood.

There's a playground in my neighborhood.

Where is it?

It's across from the bank.

☑ Read an e-mail about a neighborhood; use vocabulary for places around town **UNIT 5** **65**

LESSON E Writing

1 Before you write

A Listen. Draw the way from the train station to the school.

CLASS CD1 TK 49

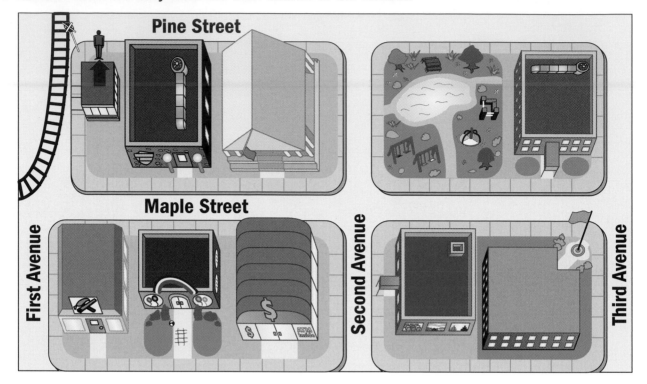

Write. Look at the map. Complete the directions from the train station to the school.

across from	go straight	on the corner of	turn right
cross	one block	straight ahead	

START
1. From the train station, turn right.

2. _____Go straight_____ on Pine Street.

3. _____ on Second Avenue.

4. Go _____.

5. _____ Maple Street. Then turn left on Maple Street.

6. Walk _____ to the corner.

7. The school is _____ Maple Street and Third Avenue.

FINISH
8. It's _____ the apartment building.

Talk with a partner. Give different directions to get from the train station to the school.

B Write. Add capital letters.

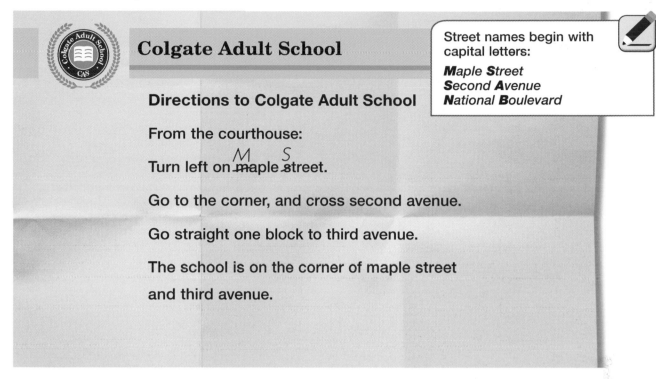

Colgate Adult School

Directions to Colgate Adult School

From the courthouse:

Turn left on ~~m~~aple ~~s~~treet.
^M ^S

Go to the corner, and cross second avenue.

Go straight one block to third avenue.

The school is on the corner of maple street

and third avenue.

Street names begin with capital letters:

Maple **S**treet
Second **A**venue
National **B**oulevard

C Write. Work with a partner. Complete the chart. Write four streets near your school. Write four places near your school.

Streets	Places

2 Write

Draw a map first. Show directions to your school. Start from a bus stop, a train station, a subway stop, a restaurant, or your home.

Write the directions to your school.

3 After you write

A Read your directions to a partner.

B Check your partner's directions.

- What are the street names?
- Do all the street names have capital letters?

LESSON F Another view

1 Life-skills reading

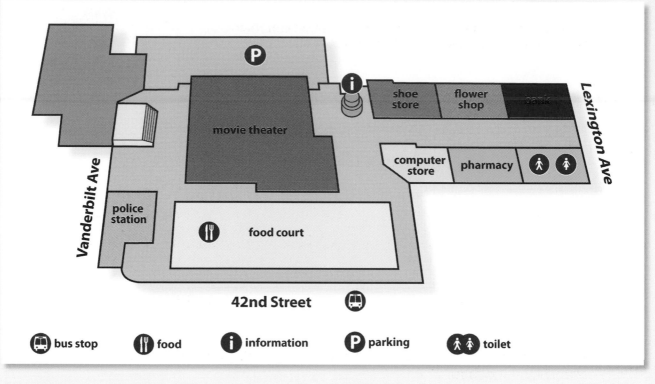

A Read the questions. Look at the map. Fill in the answer.

1. Where is the pharmacy?

   (A) It's between the shoe store and the bank.

   (B) It's on Lexington Avenue.

   (C) It's next to the computer store.

   (D) It's across from the shoe store.

2. Where is the bus stop?

   (A) It's on Lexington Avenue.

   (B) It's on 42nd Street.

   (C) It's on Vanderbilt Avenue.

   (D) It's on the corner of Lexington Avenue and 42nd Street.

3. Where is the police station?

   (A) It's on Vanderbilt Avenue.

   (B) It's next to the shoe store.

   (C) It's on Lexington Avenue.

   (D) It's on the corner of Lexington Avenue and 42nd Street.

4. Where is the flower shop?

   (A) It's next to the police station.

   (B) It's across from the computer store.

   (C) It's between the shoe store and the bank.

   (D) It's on Vanderbilt Avenue.

B Talk with your classmates. Ask and answer the questions.

1. What places in your neighborhood do you go to every week?

2. Where do you go on the weekend?

2 Grammar connections: negative imperatives

Affirmative	Negative	
Turn right on Elm Street. **Use** cell phones outside.	**Don't turn** left on Elm Street. **Don't use** cell phones in the library.	don't = do not

A Work with a partner. Match the signs and the words.

1. _e_   2. ____   3. ____

4. ____   5. ____   6. ____

a. Don't park here.

b. Don't litter.

c. Don't ride bicycles.

d. Don't use cell phones.

e. Don't turn left.

f. Don't fish.

B Work with your partner. Where do the signs go? Write the numbers from 2A on the map.

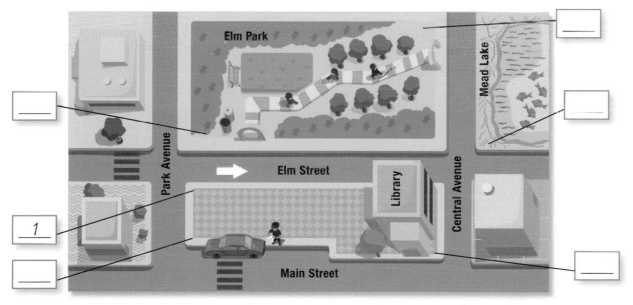

A Don't turn left on Elm Street. That's number one. That goes here.

B Don't use cell phones in . . .

3 Wrap up

Complete the **Self-assessment** on page 138.

LESSON **A**
Listening

1 Before you listen

A Look at the picture. What do you see?

B Point to a person: eating • talking • taking a nap
drinking coffee • reading a schedule • buying a snack

Unit Goals

Get information from a weekly planner

Describe own daily schedule

Interpret information on a course schedule

2 Listen

A Listen. Write the letter of the conversation.

STUDENT TK 25
CLASS CD2 TK 2

1. _____

2. _____

3. _____

4. _____

5. _____

6. _*a*_

B Listen again to the conversations. Circle the time you hear.

STUDENT TK 25
CLASS CD2 TK 2

A.	(10:30)	11:30	2:30	D.	10:15	10:45	10:40
B.	5:30	5:40	6:30	E.	10:45	12:45	2:45
C.	11:00	12:00	1:00	F.	11:30	7:30	12:30

Listen again. Check your answers.

3 After you listen

Talk with a partner. Take turns. Ask and tell the time.

What time is it?

It's ten o'clock.

1. ten o'clock   2. ten-thirty   3. six-fifteen   4. five-twenty

5. twelve-fifty   6. two-forty-five   7. seven-thirty   8. nine-oh-five

LESSON B What do you do in the evening?

1 Grammar focus: simple present; *What* questions

Questions

What	**do** you **do**	in the evening?
	does he **do**	
	does she **do**	
	do they **do**	

Answers

I	**read**.
He	**reads**.
She	**reads**.
They	**read**.

With *he* and *she*:
do → does
exercise → exercises
go → goes
study → studies
watch → watches

Turn to page 143 for a complete grammar chart.

2 Practice

A Write. Complete the sentences. Use *do* or *does* and the correct form of the verb.

1. **A** What _____do_____ they do in the evening?

   B They _____watch_____ TV.
   (watch / watches)

2. **A** What _____ he do in the afternoon?

   B He _____.
   (study / studies)

3. **A** What _____ she do in the morning?

   B She _____.
   (exercise / exercises)

4. **A** What _____ they do on Sunday?

   B They _____ to the park.
   (go / goes)

Listen and repeat. Then practice with a partner.

CLASS CD2 TK 4

B **Listen** to the Wilder family's schedule. Then listen and repeat.

SATURDAY MORNING	SATURDAY AFTERNOON	SATURDAY EVENING
Jill watches TV.	She plays soccer.	She listens to music.
Mr. and Mrs. Wilder go shopping.	They work in the garden.	They pay bills.

CLASS CD2 TK 5

Listen. Then talk with a partner. Change the **bold** words and make conversations.

> **A** What **does Jill** do on **Saturday morning**?
> **B** **She** usually **watches TV**.

1. Jill / Saturday morning
2. Mr. and Mrs. Wilder / Saturday evening
3. Mr. and Mrs. Wilder / Saturday morning
4. Jill / Saturday afternoon
5. Mr. and Mrs. Wilder / Saturday afternoon
6. Jill / Saturday evening

3 Communicate

Talk with your classmates. Ask questions about the weekend.

> What do you do on Saturday morning?
> I usually go to the grocery store.

USEFUL LANGUAGE

Usually means *most of the time.*
Always means *all of the time.*

☑ Use simple present; ask and answer *what* questions   **UNIT 6**   **73**

LESSON C I go to work at 8:00.

1 Grammar focus: *at*, *in*, and *on* with time; *When* questions

Prepositions of time

at	1:30	in	the morning	on	Saturday
	night		January		the weekend

Questions		Answers
When	**do** you **go** to work?	I **go** to work **at** 8 o'clock.
	does he **have** class?	He **has** class **on** Monday.

Turn to page 143 for a complete grammar chart.

With *he* and *she*:
have → has

2 Practice

A Write. Complete the sentences. Use *at*, *in*, or *on*.

1. I have English class _on_ Tuesday and Thursday.
2. My sister usually has class ____ Saturday.
3. I do homework ____ night.
4. My father goes to work ____ the morning.
5. He always catches the bus ____ 8:45.
6. Sometimes, my mom goes to PTA meetings ____ the evening.
7. I usually go on vacation ____ July.

PTA meetings: First Tuesday of the month

CULTURE NOTE

The PTA is the Parent-Teacher Association at a school. Parents and teachers meet in a group to talk about school.

B Write. Read the answers. Complete the questions.

1. A When ___do___ you ___go___ on vacation?

   B I usually go on vacation in July.

2. A When _____ your sister _____ class?

   B She usually has class on Saturday.

3. A When _____ your father _____ the bus?

   B He always catches the bus at 8:45.

4. A When _____ you _____ homework?

   B I always do homework at night.

Listen and repeat. Then practice with a partner.

CLASS CD2 TK 6

CLASS CD2 TK 7

C Listen. Then talk with a partner. Change the **bold** words and make conversations.

Mrs. Wilder's Schedule

SUNDAY	MONDAY	TUESDAY	WEDNESDAY	THURSDAY	FRIDAY	SATURDAY
rest	11:00 a.m. volunteer at the high school	7:30 p.m. cooking class	2:30 p.m. driving lessons	4:00 p.m. Spanish class	6:30 p.m. PTA meeting	9:00 a.m. go shopping

A When does Mrs. Wilder **volunteer at the high school**?
B She **volunteers at the high school on Monday**.
A What time?
B At **11:00 in the morning**.

CULTURE NOTE

Many people in the U.S. do volunteer work in their free time. Volunteers do not receive money for their work.

1. volunteer at the high school
2. take driving lessons
3. have cooking class
4. have Spanish class
5. go shopping
6. go to the PTA meeting

USEFUL LANGUAGE

She **has** cooking class on Tuesday.
She **goes to** cooking class on Tuesday.

3 Communicate

Write. What are five things you do every week? Make a list.

> 1. call my mother
> 2. go to English class
> 3. work
> 4. visit friends
> 5. go to the grocery store

Talk with a partner. Ask questions about your partner's list.

When do you call your mother?

I usually call my mother on Sunday at nine o'clock at night.

☑ Use prepositions (*at, in, on*) with time words; ask and answer *when* questions

LESSON **D** Reading

1 Before you read

Talk. Bob has a new job. Look at the picture.
Answer the questions.

1. What is Bob wearing?
2. What is his new job?

2 Read

 Listen and read.

STUDENT TK 26
CLASS CD2 TK 8

Meet Our New Employee: Bob Green

Please welcome Bob. He is a new security guard. He works the night shift
at the East End Factory. Bob starts work at 11:00 at night. He leaves work at
7:00 in the morning.

Bob likes these hours because he can spend time with his family. Bob
says, "I eat breakfast with my wife, Arlene, and my son, Brett, at 7:30 every
morning. I help Brett with his homework in the afternoon. I eat dinner with my
family at 6:30. Then we watch TV. At 10:30, I go to work."

Congratulations to Bob on his new job!

> To help you remember, ask
> questions as you read:
> **Who** is this reading about?
> **What** is this reading about?
> **Where** does Bob work?
> **When** does Bob work?

3 After you read

A Read the sentences. Are they correct? Circle *Yes* or *No*.

1. Bob is a new police officer.   Yes   (No)
2. He starts work at 7:00 at night.   Yes   No
3. He likes to spend time with his family.   Yes   No
4. Bob helps Brett with his homework.   Yes   No

Write. Correct the sentences.

1. Bob is a new <u>security guard</u>.

B Write. Answer the questions about Bob's schedule.

1. Where does Bob work? _____
2. Who is Arlene? _____
3. What does Bob do at 7:30 every morning? _____
4. When does the Green family watch TV? _____

4 Picture dictionary *Daily activities*

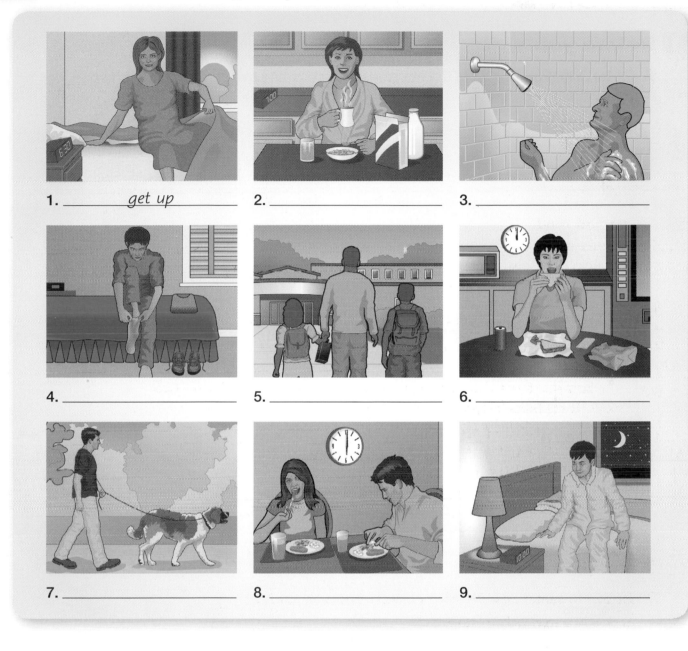

1. _____get up_____
2. _____
3. _____
4. _____
5. _____
6. _____
7. _____
8. _____
9. _____

STUDENT TK 27
CLASS CD2 TK 9

A **Write** the words in the picture dictionary. Then listen and repeat.

eat breakfast	get dressed	take a shower
eat dinner	get up	take the children to school
eat lunch	go to bed	walk the dog

B **Talk** with a partner. Ask and answer questions about your daily activities.

> When do you eat breakfast?

> I usually eat breakfast at 6:45.

☑ Read an article about a new employee; use vocabulary for daily activities **UNIT 6** 77

LESSON E Writing

1 Before you write

A Write. What do you do in the morning, afternoon, and evening?
Complete the chart.

Morning	Afternoon	Evening
get up		
get dressed		

Talk with a partner about your daily schedule.

> What do you do in the morning?

> I get up. I get dressed. . . .

Write sentences.

Morning

I get up.

I get dressed.

_____

_____

Afternoon

_____

_____

_____

_____

Evening

_____

_____

_____

_____

LESSON F Another view

1 Life-skills reading

Class Schedule: Spring Semester			
BUSINESS			
Business English	MTuWThF	5:00–7:30 p.m.	3/16–5/25
Keyboarding	MWF	1:00–3:00 p.m.	1/15–5/25
Introduction to Computers	TuTh	9:30–11:30 a.m.	3/17–5/24
Word Processing	TuTh	6:30–9:30 p.m.	3/17–5/24
ENGLISH AS A SECOND LANGUAGE			
ESL Beginning	MTuWThF	8:15–10:15 a.m.	1/15–5/25
ESL Intermediate	MTuWThF	8:15–10:15 a.m.	1/15–5/25
ESL Citizenship	Sat	8:00–10:45 a.m.	1/20–5/19
ESL Citizenship	Sun	1:45–4:30 p.m.	1/21–5/20
ESL Pronunciation	MWF	12:00–1:00 p.m.	3/16–5/25
ESL Writing	MTuWTh	12:00–1:15 p.m.	3/16–5/24

USEFUL LANGUAGE

M	Monday
T or Tu	Tuesday
W	Wednesday
Th	Thursday
F	Friday
Sat	Saturday
Sun	Sunday

A Read the questions. Look at the schedule. Fill in the answer.

1. What time does the ESL Citizenship class start on Saturday morning?
   - Ⓐ at 7:45
   - Ⓑ at 8:00
   - Ⓒ at 8:15
   - Ⓓ at 10:45

2. When does the Introduction to Computers class start?
   - Ⓐ on January 15
   - Ⓑ on March 16
   - Ⓒ on March 17
   - Ⓓ on March 19

3. When is the ESL Pronunciation class?
   - Ⓐ on Monday, Wednesday, and Friday
   - Ⓑ on Tuesday and Thursday
   - Ⓒ on Monday, Tuesday, and Thursday
   - Ⓓ on Monday, Tuesday, and Wednesday

4. When does the spring semester end?
   - Ⓐ in January
   - Ⓑ in February
   - Ⓒ in March
   - Ⓓ in May

B Talk with a partner. Ask and answer questions about the schedule.

> What time does the Business English class start?

> It starts at five o'clock.

B **Write.** Complete the paragraph. Use *in*, *on*, and *at*.

> Leave space at the beginning of a paragraph. This space is an *indent*.

Hamid
August 10

My Daily Schedule

Let me tell you about my daily schedule. <u>On</u> Monday, I usually get up ____ 6:30 ____ the morning. I eat breakfast and get dressed. ____ 8:00, I go to work. I work at a department store. I eat lunch ____ 12:30. ____ the afternoon, I take a break ____ 3:30. I finish work ____ 5:00. I go to a fast-food restaurant or a coffee shop for dinner. I get home ____ 6:45 or 7:00. I read ____ the evening. I go to bed ____ 10:00.

2 Write

Write a paragraph about your daily schedule.

3 After you write

A **Read** your paragraph to a partner.

B **Check** your partner's paragraph.

- What does your partner do in the evening?
- Is there an indent at the beginning of the paragraph?

2 Grammar connections: *start / end* and *open / close*

Use *start* and *end* for events.	Use *open* and *close* for places.
What time does the meeting **start**?	What time does the store **open**?
What time does it **end**?	What time does it **close**?

A Talk with a partner. Ask and answer questions about the notices. Take turns.

A What time does the computer club meeting *start*?

B At 5:00 p.m. What time does the library *close*?

A At 8:00 p.m.

Computer Club Meeting
Every Tuesday
5:00 p.m. – 7:30 p.m.
At the Lincoln Library
Library hours:
8:00 a.m. – 8:00 p.m.

The History of Rock Music
See a great show about rock music!
Show: 7:00 p.m. – 9:15 p.m., Wednesday
Ticket office hours:
6:00 p.m. – 11:00 p.m.

Cooking Class with Yolanda
Learn to cook with
Yolanda Gomez at Yoli's Café.
9:00 a.m. – 11:00 a.m. on Saturdays
Restaurant hours:
12:00 p.m. – 10:00 p.m.

Basketball Game
Rockets vs. Leopards
Game time: 7:30 p.m.– 10:00 p.m., Friday
Gym hours:
4:30 p.m. – 10:30 p.m.

B Talk with your partner. Write times for the signs. Then share your information with the class.

A What time does the park open?

B How about 9:00 a.m.?

A No. That's too late. How about 7:00 a.m.?

B OK. And it closes at . . .

City Park Hours
_____ to _____ every day
Free Music
_____ to _____ on Sundays

Free Beginner English Class
_____ to _____ on Fridays in Room 28
at Central Community Center
Center Hours: _____ to _____
Monday – Friday

3 Wrap up

Complete the **Self-assessment** on page 138.

Review

Read the questions. Then listen and circle the answers.

CLASS CD2 TK 10

1. Where is the DMV?
   a. on Broadway
   b. on Fifth Avenue

2. What is the address number?
   a. 550
   b. 515

3. Is the DMV between the coffee shop and the grocery store?
   a. Yes, it is.
   b. No, it isn't.

4. Is the DMV between the bank and the coffee shop?
   a. Yes, it is.
   b. No, it isn't.

5. Is the DMV across from the hospital?
   a. Yes, it is.
   b. No, it isn't.

Talk with a partner. Ask and answer the questions. Use complete sentences.

2 Grammar

A Write. Complete the story.

Kate's Day

Kate is very busy. She's a wife, a mother, and a volunteer at the library.

_____In_____ the morning, she _____ breakfast with her husband.
1. In / On   2. has / have

_____ 8:30, she takes the children to school. Her house is
3. At / In

_____ Tenth and Pine. The school is _____ the
4. on / on the corner of   5. across from / between

post office. At 3:30, Kate _____ her children from school. The family
6. get / gets

_____ dinner at 6:00. In the evening, they _____ TV.
7. eat / eats   8. watch / watches

B Write. Unscramble the words. Make questions about the story.

1. morning / Kate / do / What / does / the / in / ? _What does Kate do in the morning?_
2. school / Where / the / is / ? _____
3. get / When / children / does / her / Kate / ? _____
4. What time / the family / eat / dinner / does / ? _____

Talk with a partner. Ask and answer the questions.

3 Pronunciation: intonation in questions

A Listen to the intonation in these questions.

CLASS CD2 TK 11

> Where is the bank?

> Is the bank on Broadway?

> When is your class?

> Is your class in the morning?

B Listen and repeat.

CLASS CD2 TK 12

Wh- questions

1. **A** Where is the post office?
   B It's on First Street.

2. **A** What time do they eat dinner?
   B They eat dinner at 6:30.

Yes/No questions

3. **A** Are you from Mexico?
   B Yes, I am.

4. **A** Does he start work at 7:00?
   B No, he doesn't.

C Talk with a partner. Ask and answer the questions.

1. What time do you go to bed?
2. When is your birthday?
3. Where is your supermarket?
4. What time is your English class?
5. Do you visit your friends on the weekend?
6. Do you work in the evening?
7. Do you volunteer?
8. Do you watch TV in the afternoon?

D Write five questions.

What's your name?

1. _____
2. _____
3. _____
4. _____
5. _____

Talk with a partner. Ask and answer the questions. Use correct intonation.

> What's your name?

> My name is Teresa.

LESSON A
Listening

1 Before you listen

A Look at the picture. What do you see?

B Point to: apples • bananas • bread • cheese • cookies
milk • a cashier • a shopping cart • a stock clerk

Unit Goals	Identify food items
	Make a shopping list
	Interpret information in a supermarket ad

UNIT 7

2 Listen

A **Listen.** Write the letter of the conversation.

STUDENT TK 28
CLASS CD2 TK 13

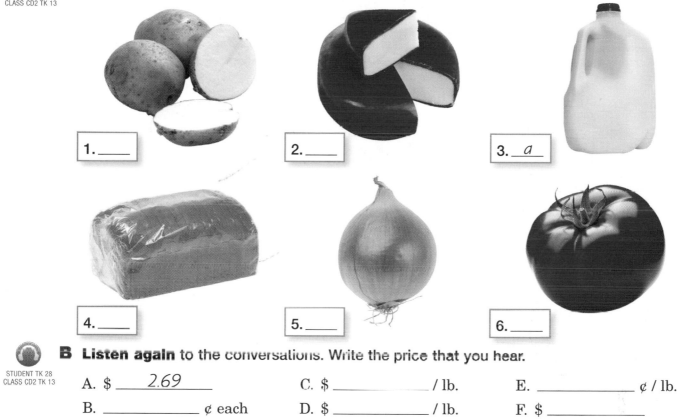

1. _____

2. _____

3. _a_

4. _____

5. _____

6. _____

B **Listen again** to the conversations. Write the price that you hear.

STUDENT TK 28
CLASS CD2 TK 13

A. $ ___2.69___   C. $ _____ / lb.   E. _____ ¢ / lb.

B. _____ ¢ each   D. $ _____ / lb.   F. $ _____

Listen again. Check your answers.

3 After you listen

Add the prices of all the items. What is the total?

Sales Receipt

bananas	3 lb	$1.98
apples	2 lb	$2.98
bread	2	$7.58
cheese	1/2 lb	$3.50
potatoes	3 lb	$2.97
milk	2	$5.38
Total		_____

USEFUL LANGUAGE

69¢ / lb. = *sixty-nine cents a pound*

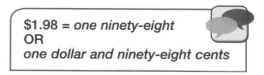

$1.98 = *one ninety-eight*
OR
one dollar and ninety-eight cents

LESSON B How many? How much?

1 Grammar focus: count / non-count nouns; How many? / How much?

Questions		Answers		
How many apples	do we need?	We need	**one apple.** **two apples.**	We don't need any.
How much milk	do we need?	We need	**a lot of milk.**	We don't need any.

Count nouns			Non-count nouns		
an apple	a cookie	an orange	bread	juice	rice
a banana	an egg	a peach	cheese	meat	sugar
a carrot	an onion	a pie	coffee	milk	water

2 Practice

A Look at the pictures. Circle only the count nouns.

1. 2. 3. 4.

5. 6. 7. 8.

9. 10. 11. 12.

Listen and repeat.

CLASS CD2 TK 14

B Write. Look at the pictures on page 86. Write the food words on the chart.

1. *carrots*	5.	9.
2. *water*	6.	10.
3.	7.	11.
4.	8.	12.

C Write. Complete the questions. Use *many* or *much*.

1. How _____*many*_____ eggs do we need?
2. How _____*much*_____ juice do we need?
3. How _____ milk do we need?
4. How _____ pies do we need?

5. How _____ bread do we need?
6. How _____ potatoes do we need?
7. How _____ rice do we need?
8. How _____ meat do we need?

CLASS CD2 TK 15

Listen and repeat.

D Talk with a partner. Change the **bold** words and make conversations.

> **A** We need some **apples**.
> **B** How **many apples** do we need?
> **A** **Two.**

> **A** We need some **milk**.
> **B** How **much milk** do we need?
> **A** **Not much.**

1. apples / two
2. milk / not much
3. bananas / five
4. bread / a lot

5. oranges / six
6. cheese / not much
7. eggs / a dozen
8. onions / not many

> **USEFUL** LANGUAGE
>
> *How many do we need?*
> You can answer *A few, Not many,* or *A lot.*
>
> *How much do we need?*
> You can answer *A little, Not much,* or *A lot.*

3 Communicate

Talk with a partner. Pretend you are making a fruit salad for four friends. Check (✓) six items. Then make conversations.

How many apples do we need?
We need three.

☐ apples   ☐ cherries   ☐ pineapples
☐ bananas   ☐ orange juice   ☐ strawberries
☐ blueberries ☐ oranges   ☐ sugar

☑ Use *how many* and *how much* with count and non-count nouns   **UNIT 7   87**

LESSON C Are there any bananas?

1 Grammar focus: *There is / There are*

Statements

There is	a banana	on the table.
There are	two bananas	
There is	bread	on the table.

Questions

Is there	a banana	on the table?
Are there	any bananas	
Is there	any bread	on the table?

Answers

		is.		isn't.
Yes, **there**			No, **there**	
		are.		aren't.
Yes, **there**	is.		No, **there**	isn't.

2 Practice

A **Write.** Complete the sentences. Use *there is*, *there are*, *there isn't*, or *there aren't*.

1. **A** Is there any bread on the table?
   B Yes, _____*there is*_____.

2. **A** Are there any eggs?
   B No, _____.

3. **A** Is there any juice?
   B Yes, _____.

4. **A** Is there any water?
   B No, _____.

5. **A** Are there any cookies?
   B Yes, _____.

6. **A** Are there any bananas?
   B No, _____.

Listen and repeat. Then practice with a partner.

CLASS CD2 TK 16

B **Write.** Complete the questions. Use *Is there* or *Are there*.

1. **A** _____ _____ any meat in the refrigerator?
   B Yes, there is.

2. **A** _____ _____ any oranges?
   B Yes, there are.

3. **A** _____ _____ any cheese?
   B No, there isn't.

4. **A** _____ _____ any coffee?
   B Yes, there is.

5. **A** _____ _____ any apples?
   B No, there aren't.

6. **A** _____ _____ any cherries?
   B Yes, there are.

Listen and repeat. Then practice with a partner.

CLASS CD2 TK 17

C Write. Complete the sentences. Use *There is* or *There are*.

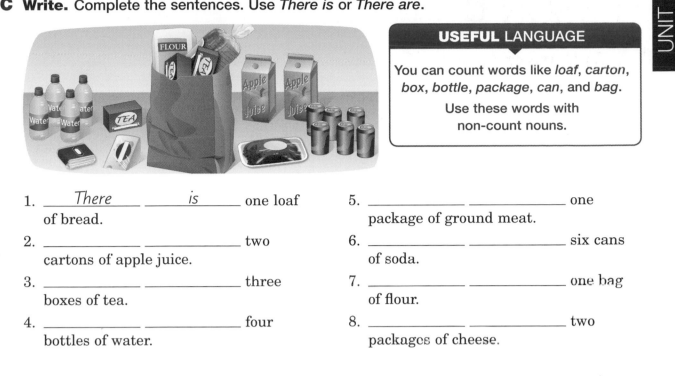

1. ___There___ ___is___ one loaf of bread.

2. _____ _____ two cartons of apple juice.

3. _____ _____ three boxes of tea.

4. _____ _____ four bottles of water.

5. _____ _____ one package of ground meat.

6. _____ _____ six cans of soda.

7. _____ _____ one bag of flour.

8. _____ _____ two packages of cheese.

CLASS CD2 TK 18

Listen and repeat.

D Talk with a partner. Look at the picture. Make conversations.

Is there any rice?

Yes, there is a bag of rice on the shelf.

Is there any soda?

No, there isn't.

1. rice	3. milk	5. tea	7. sugar	9. flour
2. soda	4. coffee	6. cheese	8. water	10. meat

3 Communicate

Talk with a partner. Ask and answer these questions.

1. What's in your refrigerator?
2. What's on your kitchen shelves?

LESSON D Reading

1 Before you read

Talk. Shirley and Dan are shopping.
Look at the picture. Answer the questions.

1. Where are they?
2. What are they doing?

2 Read

Listen and read.

STUDENT TK 29
CLASS CD2 TK 19

Regular Customers

Shirley and Dan are regular customers at SaveMore Supermarket. They go to SaveMore three or four times a week. The cashiers and stock clerks at SaveMore know them and like them. There are fruit and vegetables, meat and fish, and cookies and cakes in the supermarket. But today, Shirley and Dan are buying apples, bananas, bread, and cheese. There is one problem. The total is $16.75. They only have a ten-dollar bill, 5 one-dollar bills, and three quarters!

> When you don't understand a word, look for clues.
>
> Do you understand *regular customer*?
>
> Clue: They go to SaveMore *three or four times a week.*

3 After you read

A Read the sentences. Are they correct? Circle *Yes* or *No.*

1. Shirley and Dan go to SaveMore three or
   four times a day.   Yes   (No)

2. They are regular customers at SaveMore
   Supermarket.   Yes   No

3. The cashiers and stock clerks know them.   Yes   No

4. Shirley and Dan are buying meat and fish.   Yes   No

5. Shirley and Dan have $16.00.   Yes   No

B Write. Correct the sentences.

1. Shirley and Dan go to SaveMore three or four times a <u>week</u>.

C Write. Answer the questions about Shirley and Dan.

1. How much money do Shirley and Dan have? _____
2. How many quarters do they have? _____
3. How much more money do they need? _____

4 Picture dictionary Money

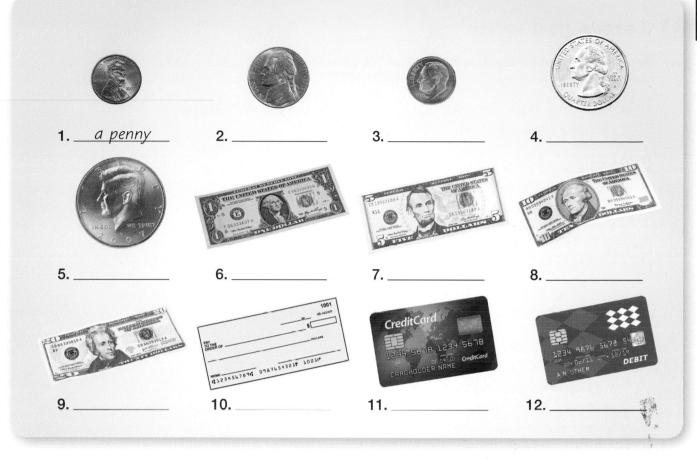

1. _a penny_
2. _____
3. _____
4. _____
5. _____
6. _____
7. _____
8. _____
9. _____
10. _____
11. _____
12. _____

STUDENT TK 30
CLASS CD2 TK 20

A **Write** the words in the picture dictionary. Then listen and repeat.

a check	a dime	a nickel	a quarter
a credit card	a five-dollar bill	a one-dollar bill	a ten-dollar bill
a debit card	a half-dollar	a penny	a twenty-dollar bill

B **Talk** with a partner. Look at the pictures.
Change the **bold** words and make conversations.

A Do you have change for a **dollar**?
B Sure. What do you need?
A I need **four quarters**.
B Here you are.

You can say:
a one-dollar bill OR *a dollar*
a five-dollar bill OR *five dollars*
a ten-dollar bill OR *ten dollars*

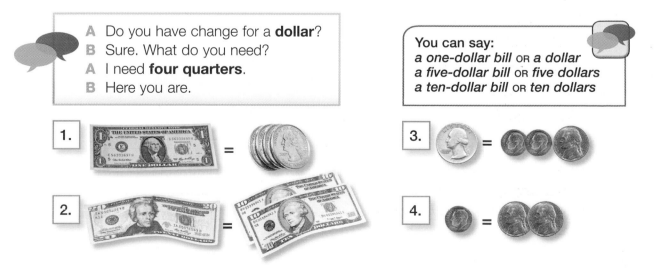

☑ Read a paragraph about supermarket customers; identify money and types of payment   **UNIT 7**   **91**

LESSON E Writing

 Before you write

A **Talk** with a partner. Ask and answer questions.

1. When do you go shopping?
2. What are the names of some supermarkets in your neighborhood?
3. What do you usually buy at the supermarket?

B **Read** the note. Make a shopping list.

> Mom,
>
> Please stop at SaveMore on your way home. I'm making spaghetti for dinner.
>
> There is cheese in the refrigerator. There are two peppers next to the stove, but there aren't any onions. Please get two. I also need four carrots, six tomatoes, a carton of milk, and a package of ground meat.
>
> Thanks.
>
> Kate

Going shopping:
2 onions
_____
_____
_____
_____

C **Write.** Look at the picture. What is she buying? Write the words.

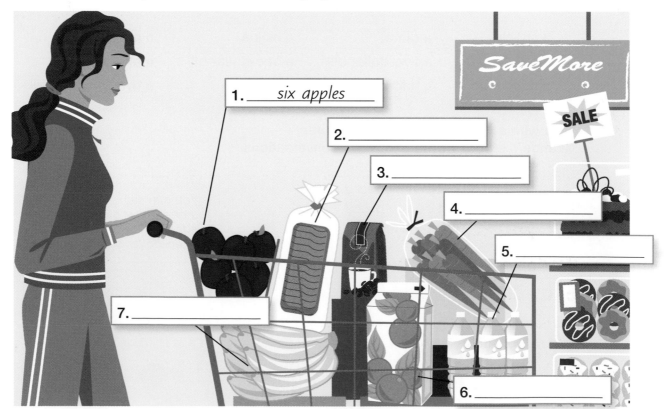

1. six apples
2. _____
3. _____
4. _____
5. _____
6. _____
7. _____

D **Write.** Correct the note. Add commas.

Hi Roberto,

    I'm making dinner tonight, but I need a few more groceries. I need a package of meat, an onion a green pepper three tomatoes and a bag of rice. I also need a carton of milk two bottles of apple juice six cans of soda and a carton of orange juice. Oh, and one more thing – a dozen eggs.

    Thanks. See you tonight.

                                 Iris

> Put a comma (,) after each item when there is a list of three or more items.
> *Please buy five oranges, two apples, and a peach.*

2 Write

Write a note asking someone to go shopping for you.

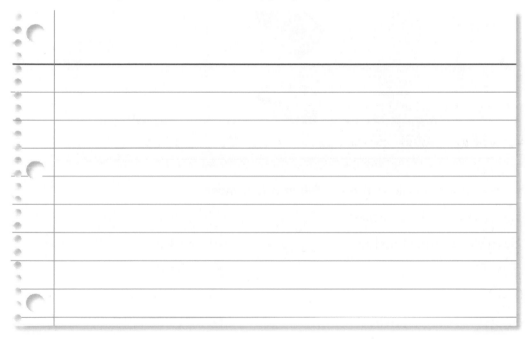

3 After you write

A **Read** your note to a partner.

B **Check** your partner's note.

- What food does your partner need?
- Are the commas correct?

LESSON A
Listening

1 Before you listen

A Look at the picture. What do you see?

B Point to: a server • a busperson • a cashier • a cook
an electrician • a nurse • a nursing assistant
• a construction worker

Red Oak Cafe

Mai Linh

Unit Goals

Identify common jobs

Describe skills

Complete a job application

2 Listen

A **Listen.** Write the letter of the conversation.

STUDENT TK 31
CLASS CD2 TK 21

1. ____

2. ____

3. ____

4. _a_

5. ____

6. ____

B **Listen again** to the conversations. Write the years or dates you hear.

STUDENT TK 31
CLASS CD2 TK 21

A. from ___1998___ to ___2010___

B. from _____ to _____

C. from _____ to _____

D. from _____ to _____

E. in _____

F. _____ years ago

Listen again. Check your answers.

3 After you listen

Where do the people work? Write the words.

busperson   cashier   doctor   nurse   receptionist   server

1. ___doctor___

2. _____

3. _____

hospital

4. _____

5. _____

6. _____

restaurant

LESSON B I was a teacher.

Grammar focus: simple past of *be*

Questions

Were	you	a student?
Was	he	a student?
Was	she	a student?
Were	they	students?

Answers

	I **was**.	
Yes,	he **was**.	
	she **was**.	
	they **were**.	

	I **wasn't**. I **was** a teacher.
	he **wasn't**. He **was** a teacher.
No,	she **wasn't**. She **was** a teacher.
	they **weren't**. They **were** teachers.

Turn to page 144 for a complete grammar chart.

wasn't = was not | weren't = were not

2 Practice

A Write. Look at the pictures. Complete the sentences. Use *is*, *are*, *was*, or *were*.

APPLICATION FORM

Amy Cho

Job History:

2006–Present   Nurse

2000–2006   Teacher

1. She _____*was*_____ a teacher before.

   Now she _____*is*_____ a nurse.

2. She _____ a manager now.

   She _____ a cashier before.

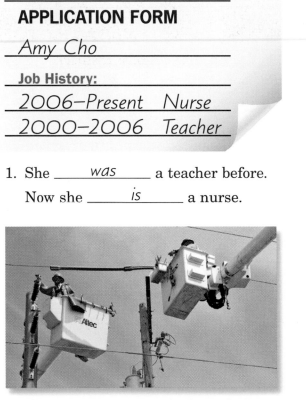

Job Application

Name: | Ben Liao

Job History: | 2006-Present Construction Worker

| 2004-2006 Server

3. They _____ students before.

   Now they _____ electricians.

4. He _____ a server before.

   Now he _____ a construction worker.

Listen and repeat.

B Talk with a partner. Look at the pictures. Change the **bold** words and make conversations.

1. **A** Was **she** a **teacher**?

   B Yes, **she** was.

2. **A** Were they **receptionists**?

   B No, they weren't. They were **nurses**.

1. a teacher?

2. receptionists?

3. a server?

4. doctors?

5. a cook?

6. a cashier?

3 Communicate

Talk with three classmates. Complete the chart.

A Sylvia, what do you do now?
B Now? I'm a homemaker.
A Oh, really? Were you a homemaker before?
B No, I wasn't. I was a receptionist in a bank.

USEFUL LANGUAGE

In conversation, *What do you do?* means *What's your job?* OR *What's your occupation?*

Name	Job now	Job before
Sylvia	a homemaker	a receptionist

Write two sentences about your classmates. Use information from the chart.

Sylvia is a homemaker now. She was a receptionist before.

☑ Use simple past of *be* (*was, were*); ask and answer *yes / no* questions **UNIT 8** **99**

LESSON C Can you cook?

1 Grammar focus: *can*

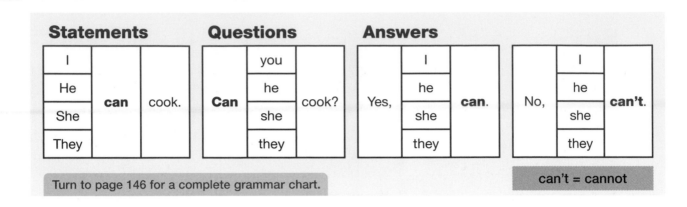

Statements		
I		
He	**can**	cook.
She		
They		

Questions		
Can	you	cook?
	he	
	she	
	they	

Answers		
Yes,	I	**can**.
	he	
	she	
	they	

No,	I	**can't**.
	he	
	she	
	they	

Turn to page 146 for a complete grammar chart.

can't = cannot

2 Practice

A Write. Complete the sentences. Use *yes*, *no*, *can*, or *can't*.

1. **A** Can she speak Spanish?
   B __Yes__, she __can__.

2. **A** Can he drive a truck?
   B __No__, he __can't__.

3. **A** Can he fix a car?
   B _____, he _____.

4. **A** Can she paint a house?
   B _____, she _____.

5. **A** Can they work with computers?
   B _____, they _____.

6. **A** Can you cook?
   B _____, I _____.

Listen and repeat. Then practice with a partner.

CLASS CD2 TK 23

B **Write.** Look at the pictures. Complete the sentences.

build things	paint	take care of children
fix cars	sell things	take care of plants

1. A painter can
   paint .

2. A salesperson can
   _____ .

3. A carpenter can
   _____ .

4. A gardener can
   _____ .

5. A child-care worker can
   _____ .

6. An auto mechanic can
   _____ .

Listen and repeat.

CLASS CD2 TK 24

C **Talk** with a partner. Look at the pictures in 2B. Change the **bold** words and make conversations.

> **A** Hi. I'm looking for a job. Can you help me?
> **B** What can you do?
> **A** I'm a **painter**. I can **paint** very well.

3 Communicate

Talk with a partner. Ask and answer questions.

What can you do?

I can cook. I can work with computers.

LESSON D Reading

Harmon Hills Nursing Home

1 Before you read

Talk. Mai Linh is looking for a new job. Look at the picture. Answer the questions.

1. Who are the people in the picture?
2. Where are they?
3. What is Mai Linh's volunteer job now?

2 Read

STUDENT TK 32
CLASS CD2 TK 25

Listen and read.

> Verb forms can tell you if something happened in the past or is happening now. *Mai Linh was a teacher in Vietnam. She is looking for a new job.*

VALLEY ADULT SCHOOL

Dear Ms. Carter:

    I am writing this letter to recommend my student Mai Linh Lam.

    Mai Linh was a teacher in Vietnam. She is looking for a new job in the United States. She is a certified nursing assistant now. She volunteers in a nursing home Monday through Friday from 12:00 to 4:30. She takes care of senior citizens.

    Mai Linh has many good skills. She can write reports. She can help elderly people move around and sit down. She can help them eat. She can also speak English and Vietnamese. These skills are useful in her job, and she is very good at her work.

Sincerely,

Elaine Maxwell

Elaine Maxwell

3 After you read

A Read the sentences. Are they correct? Circle *Yes* or *No*.

1. Mai Linh is looking for a job in Vietnam.   Yes   (No)
2. She volunteers in a hospital.   Yes   No
3. She can write reports.   Yes   No
4. She finishes work at 8:30.   Yes   No
5. She is good at her job.   Yes   No

Write. Correct the sentences.

1. Mai Linh is looking for a job in <u>the United States</u>.

B Write. Answer the questions about Mai Linh.

1. What was Mai Linh's job before? _____

2. Is Mai Linh certified? _____

3. What are her work skills? _____

> ### CULTURE NOTE
>
> For some jobs, you need a certificate. You have to take a test to get the certificate.
>
> *I'm certified* means *I have a certificate.*

4 Picture dictionary Occupations

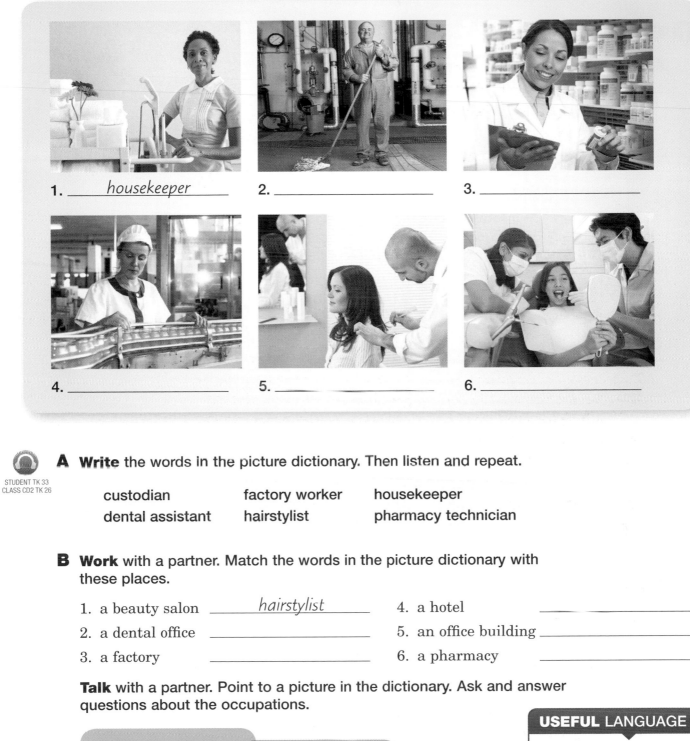

1. ___housekeeper___

2. _____

3. _____

4. _____

5. _____

6. _____

STUDENT TK 33
CLASS CD2 TK 26

A **Write** the words in the picture dictionary. Then listen and repeat.

custodian	factory worker	housekeeper
dental assistant	hairstylist	pharmacy technician

B **Work** with a partner. Match the words in the picture dictionary with these places.

1. a beauty salon ___hairstylist___

2. a dental office _____

3. a factory _____

4. a hotel _____

5. an office building _____

6. a pharmacy _____

Talk with a partner. Point to a picture in the dictionary. Ask and answer questions about the occupations.

What's her occupation?

She's a housekeeper.

Where does she work?

She works in a hotel.

USEFUL LANGUAGE

occupation = job

☑ Read a recommendation letter; use vocabulary for occupations **UNIT 8** 103

LESSON Writing

1 Before you write

A Write. Check (✓) what you can do.

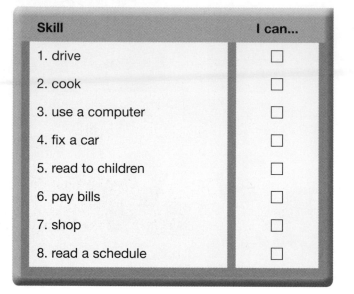

Skill	I can...
1. drive	☐
2. cook	☐
3. use a computer	☐
4. fix a car	☐
5. read to children	☐
6. pay bills	☐
7. shop	☐
8. read a schedule	☐

Talk with a partner.

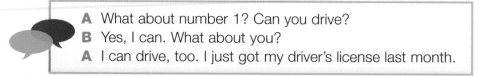

A What about number 1? Can you drive?
B Yes, I can. What about you?
A I can drive, too. I just got my driver's license last month.

B Read. Answer the questions.

> **New Message**
>
> From: Carla
> To: Ventures
> Subject: My Skills
>
> My name is Carla. I am a homemaker. I work at home. I have many skills. I can do housework. I can drive a car, and I can fix a car, too. I can speak two languages. I can cook tasty meals for my family. I can help my children with their homework, and I can use a computer.

1. What are Carla's skills? _____

_____

2. What can Carla do that you can do, too? _____

_____

2 Write

A **Write** about your occupation. Complete the sentences.

I am a _____ .

I work at _____ .

B **Write.** What are your skills? Make a list.

_____

_____

_____

_____

_____

_____

C **Write** a paragraph about your skills.

_____

_____

_____

_____

_____

_____

_____

_____

_____

_____

_____

3 After you write

A **Read** your paragraph to a partner.

B **Check** your partner's paragraph.

- What are your partner's skills?
- Is the spelling correct?

Check your spelling. Use a dictionary if necessary. Correct spelling is important in writing.

LESSON **F** Another view

APPLICATION FOR EMPLOYMENT

1. Name _____	2. Soc. Sec. No. *000-99-9103*
3. Address _____	4. Phone _____
_____	
5. Are you 16 years or older? Yes ___ No ___	6. Position desired _____

EMPLOYMENT HISTORY (List most recent job first.)

Dates	Employer Name and Address	Position
7.		
8.		
9.		

10. Important: Show your Social Security card at the time you present this application.

A **Read** the questions. Look at the job application. Fill in the answer.

1. Where do you write the job you want?

   (A) line 5
   (B) line 6
   (C) line 8
   (D) line 10

2. Where do you write your most recent job?

   (A) line 5
   (B) line 7
   (C) line 8
   (D) line 9

3. What do you show with your application?

   (A) a library card
   (B) a photograph
   (C) a driver's license
   (D) a Social Security card

4. Where do you write your phone number?

   (A) line 4
   (B) line 5
   (C) line 8
   (D) line 9

B **Write.** Complete the form with your own information.

C **Talk** with a partner about your form.

> My name is Mario Rivera. My address is 613 Apple Road, Los Angeles, California. I'm looking for a job. The job I want is construction worker.

2 Grammar connections: *be* with *and* and *but*

Use *and* to show things that are the same.	Use *but* to show things that are different.
Sid **is** at work today, **and** he **was** at work yesterday.	Natt **is** at work today, **but** she **wasn't** at work yesterday.
Ana **isn't** at work today, **and** she **wasn't** at work yesterday.	Len and Eva **aren't** at work today, **but** they **were** at work yesterday.

A **Work** with a partner. Look at the pictures. Talk about the people. Take turns.

   A John *is* at work today, *and* he *was* at work yesterday.

   B Carmen *is* at work today, *but* she *wasn't* at work yesterday.

B **Talk** in a group. Tell about your classmates. Take turns.

Mario: I'm here today, but I wasn't here yesterday.

Ina: Mario is here today, but he wasn't here yesterday. I'm here today, and I was here yesterday.

Bing: Mario is here today, but he wasn't here yesterday. Ina is here today, and she was here yesterday. I'm here . . .

3 Wrap up

Complete the **Self-assessment** on page 139.

Review

1 Listening

Read the questions. Then listen and circle the answers.

CLASS CD2 TK 27

1. What did Carlos do before?
   a. He was an office worker.
   b. He was a construction worker.

2. What does Carlos do now?
   a. He is an office worker.
   b. He is a construction worker.

3. When does Carlos buy groceries?
   a. every Tuesday
   b. every Thursday

4. Where is Carlos right now?
   a. at SaveMore Supermarket
   b. at work

5. What is he buying at the supermarket?
   a. milk, tea, bread, and eggs
   b. milk, cheese, bread, and eggs

6. How much are the groceries?
   a. $11.75
   b. $7.75

Talk with a partner. Ask and answer the questions. Use complete sentences.

2 Grammar

A **Write.** Complete the story.

Peter

Peter ____was____ a server in his country. Now he _____ a
      1. is / was   2. is / was

cashier. He can do many things. He _____ use a cash register.
                         3. can / can't

He _____ use a computer, too. But Peter has two problems.
    4. can / can't

First, he _____ speak English well. Second, he works a lot of
      5. can / can't

hours. He _____ find time to go to school.
      6. can / can't

B **Write.** Unscramble the words. Make questions about the story.

1. a / teacher / Was / Peter / country / his / in / ? _Was Peter a teacher in his country?_

2. use / cash register / a / Can / he / ? _____

3. speak / well / English / Can / he / ? _____

4. he / construction worker / Is / now / a / ? _____

Talk with a partner. Ask and answer the questions.

3 Pronunciation: the -s ending with plural nouns

A Listen to the -s ending in these plural nouns.

CLASS CD2 TK 28

/s/	/z/	/ɪz/
cakes	tomatoes	peaches
hairstylists	electricians	nurses

B Listen and repeat.

CLASS CD2 TK 29

/s/	/z/	/ɪz/
assistants	bananas	nurses
cooks	cashiers	oranges
students	drivers	packages
mechanics	cookies	boxes
receptionists	servers	peaches
books	teachers	sandwiches

Talk with a partner. Take turns. Practice the words. Make sentences with the words.

C Listen. Complete the chart.

CLASS CD2 TK 30

1. bags
2. bottles
3. clerks

4. dimes
5. pages
6. carrots

7. desks
8. languages
9. glasses

/s/	/z/	/ɪz/
	bags	

D Talk with a partner. Ask and answer the question. Use correct pronunciation.

What's in your refrigerator?

There are ____ ____.

There is _____.

LESSON A
Listening

1 Before you listen

A Look at the picture. What do you see?

B Point to a person: cleaning the bathroom • emptying the trash
mopping the floor • vacuuming the rug • ironing clothes

2 Listen

STUDENT TK 34
CLASS CD2 TK 31

A **Listen.** Write the letter of the conversation.

1. _____

2. _____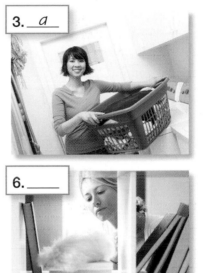

3. _a_

4. _____

5. _____

6. _____

STUDENT TK 34
CLASS CD2 TK 31

B **Listen again** to the conversations. Circle the time expression you hear.

A. (last night)	last week	last weekend
B. the day before yesterday	yesterday	yesterday morning
C. last night	yesterday	the day before yesterday
D. yesterday morning	every day last week	yesterday
E. yesterday	yesterday morning	the day before yesterday
F. last night	last weekend	last week

Listen again. Check your answers.

3 After you listen

Work with a partner. Put the words from the box in the correct category.

a bill	the floor	a shirt	the trash
a dress	the rug	a ticket	the wastebasket

iron	empty	vacuum	pay
a dress			

LESSON **B** I cleaned the living room.

Statements

I				I		
You				You		
He	**cleaned**	the living room.		He	**didn't clean**.	
She				She		
They				They		

Spelling changes
dry ➝ dried
empty ➝ emptied
mop ➝ mopped

didn't = did not

Questions

	you		
Did	he	**clean**	yesterday?
	she		
	they		

Answers

		I				I	
Yes,		he	**did**.	No,		he	**didn't**.
		she				she	
		they				they	

Time words
yesterday
the day before
    yesterday
last night
last week

Turn to page 145 for a complete grammar chart.

2 Practice

A Write. Look at the picture. Complete the sentences.

1. Yousef _____*cooked*_____ dinner.
   (cook)

2. He ___*didn't clean*___ the kitchen.
   (clean)

3. He _____ the shelves.
   (dust)

4. He _____ the dishes.
   (wash)

5. He _____ the shirts.
   (iron)

6. He _____ the trash.
   (empty)

Listen and repeat.

CLASS CD2 TK 32

B **Write.** Look at the picture. Answer the questions.

1. **A** Did Mr. Ramirez mop the floor?

   B _____ *Yes, he did.* _____

2. **A** Did Mrs. Ramirez empty the trash?

   B _____

3. **A** Did Mr. and Mrs. Ramirez wash the dishes?

   B _____

4. **A** Did Roberto dry the dishes?

   B _____

5. **A** Did Luis vacuum the rug?

   B _____

6. **A** Did Monica vacuum the rug?

   B _____

Listen and repeat. Then practice with a partner.

CLASS CD2 TK 33

3 Communicate

Talk with your classmates. Write their names on the chart.

Anna, did you cook dinner last night?

Yes, I did.

Find a classmate who:	Classmate's name
cooked dinner last night	
emptied the trash yesterday	
washed the dishes every night last week	
dried the dishes the day before yesterday	
vacuumed last weekend	
ironed clothes last week	

LESSON C I paid the bills.

1 Grammar focus: simple past with irregular verbs

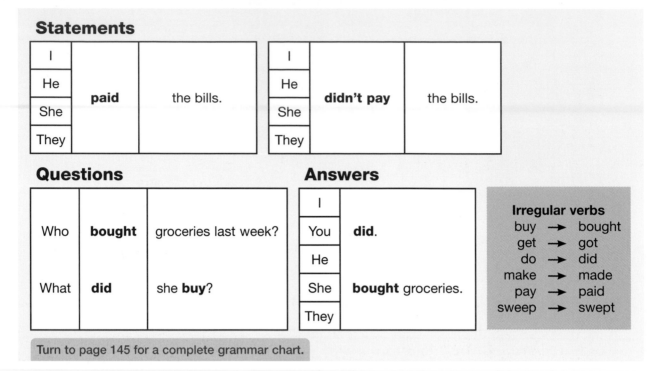

Statements

I He She They	**paid**	the bills.

I He She They	**didn't pay**	the bills.

Questions

Who	**bought**	groceries last week?
What	**did**	she **buy**?

Answers

I You He	**did**.
She They	**bought** groceries.

Irregular verbs

buy	→	bought
get	→	got
do	→	did
make	→	made
pay	→	paid
sweep	→	swept

Turn to page 145 for a complete grammar chart.

2 Practice

A Write. Look at the pictures. Complete the sentences.

Last night, Linda had to pay the bills. But first, she ___*bought*___ groceries

1. buy

after work. She _____ $15. She _____ home, and she _____

2. pay   3. get   4. make

dinner. She _____ soup and salad. After dinner, she was very tired. She

5. make

_____ the kitchen floor, but she _____ the bills!

6. sweep   7. not pay

Listen and check your answers.

B **Write.** Look at the notes. Answer the questions.

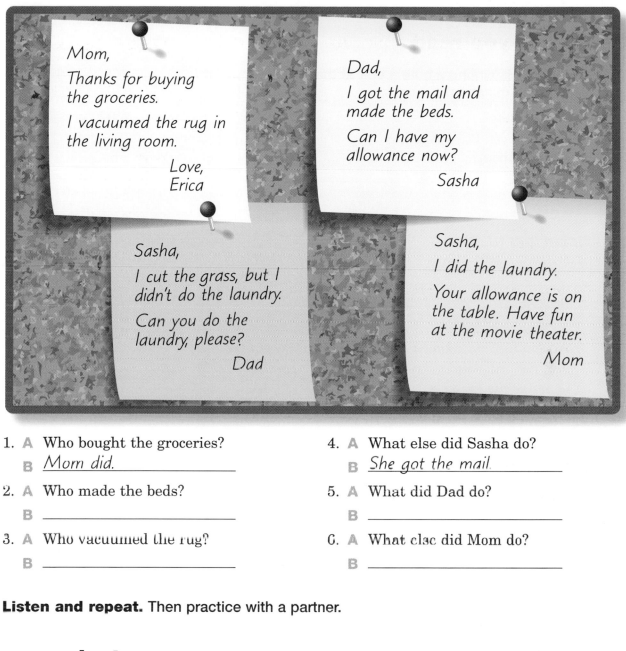

Mom,
Thanks for buying the groceries.
I vacuumed the rug in the living room.
Love,
Erica

Dad,
I got the mail and made the beds.
Can I have my allowance now?
Sasha

Sasha,
I cut the grass, but I didn't do the laundry.
Can you do the laundry, please?
Dad

Sasha,
I did the laundry.
Your allowance is on the table. Have fun at the movie theater.
Mom

1. **A** Who bought the groceries?
   B *Mom did.*

2. **A** Who made the beds?
   B _____

3. **A** Who vacuumed the rug?
   B _____

4. **A** What else did Sasha do?
   B *She got the mail.*

5. **A** What did Dad do?
   B _____

6. **A** What else did Mom do?
   B _____

Listen and repeat. Then practice with a partner.

CLASS CD2 TK 35

3 Communicate

Talk with a partner. What chores did you do yesterday? Check (✓) the boxes.

☐ paid the bills   ☐ did the laundry   ☐ swept the floor   ☐ washed the dishes
☐ bought the groceries   ☐ made the bed   ☐ got the mail   ☐ vacuumed the rug

Work in a group. Ask and answer questions.

Who paid the bills yesterday?
I did.
I didn't.

☑ Use the simple past with irregular verbs   **UNIT 9**   **115**

LESSON D Reading

 1 Before you read

Talk. Mark is writing a note. Look at the picture. Answer the questions.

1. Where is he?
2. What do you think Mark is writing about?

2 Read

 Listen and read.

STUDENT TK 35
CLASS CD2 TK 36

> Dear Karen,
>
>   Welcome home! We were very busy today. Jeff ironed the clothes. Chris emptied the trash. Sharon mopped the floor. Ben vacuumed the rug and dusted the furniture. The house is clean for you!
>
>   I cooked dinner. There is food on the stove.
>
>   Your husband,
>   Mark

> Good readers ask themselves questions before they start reading, such as *Who wrote the letter?*

3 After you read

A **Read** the sentences. Are they correct? Circle *Yes* or *No*.

1. Jeff washed the clothes.   Yes   (No)
2. Sharon swept the floor.   Yes   No
3. Ben vacuumed the rug.   Yes   No
4. Karen cooked dinner.   Yes   No
5. Chris emptied the trash.   Yes   No

Write. Correct the sentences.

1. Jeff ironed the clothes.

B **Write.** Answer the questions about the note.

1. Who dusted the furniture? _____

2. Did Sharon empty the trash? _____

3. Who is Karen? _____

116   UNIT 9

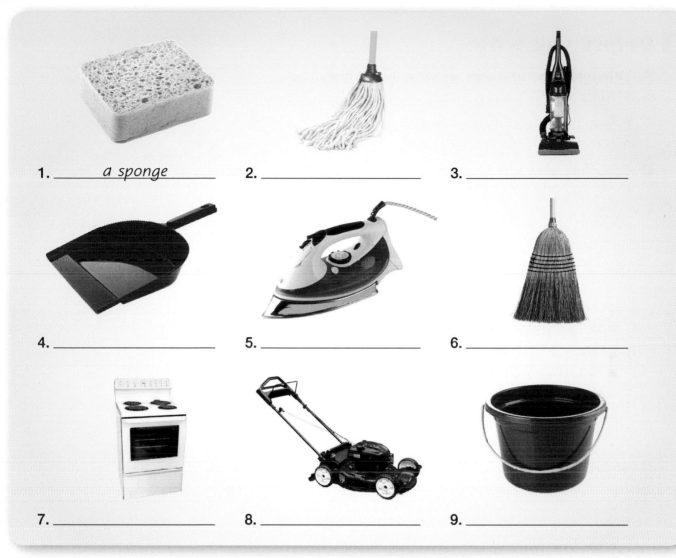

4 Picture dictionary *Household objects*

UNIT 9

1. _a sponge_ 2. _____ 3. _____

4. _____ 5. _____ 6. _____

7. _____ 8. _____ 9. _____

A Write the words in the picture dictionary. Then listen and repeat.

STUDENT TK 36
CLASS CD2 TK 37

a broom   an iron   a sponge
a bucket   a lawn mower   a stove
a dustpan   a mop   a vacuum cleaner

B Write. Match the objects with the actions.

1. an iron _d_   a. vacuum
2. a sponge ____   b. sweep
3. a stove ____   c. mop
4. a lawn mower ____ d. iron
5. a mop ____   e. cook
6. a vacuum cleaner ____ f. wash
7. a broom ____   g. cut grass

☑ Read a letter about family chores; identify household objects to use for chores   **UNIT 9**   **117**

LESSON **E** Writing

 1 Before you write

A Talk with a partner. Ask and answer the questions.

1. Who does the chores in your home? What chores?
2. Are there special times to do those chores?
3. What is your favorite chore?

B Talk. Interview three classmates. Write two chores each person did last week and one chore they didn't do.

Name	Chores you did	Chores you didn't do
Katia	bought the groceries walked the dog	didn't vacuum the rugs

C Write. Complete the note. Use the simple past form of the verbs.

Dear Mom,

I ____bought____ milk from the supermarket. It's in the refrigerator. I also
     1. buy

_____ the shelves and _____ the floor, but I didn't _____
   2. dust   3. sweep   4. wash

the dishes. Did you _____ a new sponge? Did you _____ the rug
        5. buy   6. vacuum

yesterday? I also _____ my bed.
       7. make

See you later,

Irina

D **Write.** Complete the note. Use the correct simple past form.

buy	cook	dry	mop	pay	sweep	walk	wash

Hi Tom,

   I ___cooked___ dinner for you. It's on the stove. I _____ the dishes, but I didn't _____ them. Sorry, I didn't have time. I _____ a new broom at the store. I _____ the kitchen floor with it. I _____ the floor, too, with the new mop. I didn't _____ the dog.

   Did you _____ the bills? It's the end of the month. Please remember. I'll see you tonight.

                                                     Love,

                                                     Mary

> Check your past verb forms. Use the chart on page 145.

2 Write

Write a note to a family member. Write the chores you did and didn't do.

3 After you write

A **Read** your note to a partner.

B **Check** your partner's note.

- What are two chores your partner wrote about?
- Are the past verb forms correct?

☑ Write a note about household chores   **UNIT 9**   **119**

LESSON F Another view

1 Life-skills reading

<table>
<tr><td colspan="4" style="text-align:center">**SaveMore** Supermarket   **JOB DUTIES**</td></tr>
<tr><th>Duties</th><th>Employee</th><th>Initials</th><th>Time Completed</th></tr>
<tr><td>Sweep the floor.</td><td>Joshua Liu</td><td>JL</td><td>9:15 p.m.</td></tr>
<tr><td>Mop the floor.</td><td>Kim Casey</td><td>KC</td><td>9:30 p.m.</td></tr>
<tr><td>Mop the floor.</td><td>Roger Brown</td><td>RB</td><td>9:30 p.m.</td></tr>
<tr><td>Clean the bathroom.</td><td>Ann Hamilton</td><td>AH</td><td>8:30 p.m.</td></tr>
<tr><td>Empty the trash cans.</td><td>Steve Johnson</td><td>SJ</td><td>8:45 p.m.</td></tr>
<tr><td>Turn off the lights.</td><td>Victor Morales</td><td>VM</td><td>10:00 p.m.</td></tr>
<tr><td>Lock the doors.</td><td>Victor Morales</td><td>VM</td><td>10:00 p.m.</td></tr>
</table>

A Read the questions. Look at the chart. Fill in the answer.

1. Who swept the floor?

   (A) Ann

   (B) Victor

   (C) Kim and Roger

   (D) Joshua

2. When did Steve empty the trash cans?

   (A) at 8:30 p.m.

   (B) at 8:45 p.m.

   (C) at 9:15 p.m.

   (D) at 10:00 p.m.

3. Did Victor turn off the lights?

   (A) Yes, he did.

   (B) No, he didn't. He swept the floor.

   (C) No, he didn't. He cleaned the bathroom.

   (D) No, he didn't. He mopped the floor.

4. Who mopped the floor?

   (A) Kim and Victor

   (B) Steve and Joshua

   (C) Ann and Roger

   (D) Kim and Roger

B Talk with a partner. Ask and answer questions about the chart.

Who locked the doors? — Victor did.

Did Steve empty the trash? — Yes, he did.

What did Ann do? — She cleaned the bathroom.

2 Grammar connections: *or* questions

> **Use *or* when there are two choices in a question.**
>
> Does Juan usually wash **or** sweep the floor?
> He usually sweeps the floor.

A Work with a partner. Talk about the pictures. Ask and answer. Take turns.

A Does Feng usually wash *or* dry the dishes?

B He usually washes the dishes.

A Does Mei usually wash *or* dry the dishes?

B She usually dries the dishes.

1. Feng | Mei
2. Santiago | Monica
3. Donna | Tina
4. Paco | Ivan
5. Angie | Tommy
6. Donald | Teresa

B Talk with your partner. Ask and answer. Take turns.

> Do you usually wash the dishes or use a dishwasher?
>
> I usually wash the dishes.

1. wash the dishes / use a dishwasher
2. eat lunch at home / have lunch at work
3. stay home on the weekends / go out on the weekends
4. wash your clothes at home / go to the laundromat
5. mop the floors / vacuum the rugs

3 Wrap up

Complete the **Self-assessment** on page 140.

☑ Scan for information on a job duties chart; ask and answer *or* questions   **UNIT 9   121**

LESSON A
Listening

1 Before you listen

A Look at the picture. What do you see?

B Point to these activities: camping • fishing • hiking
canoeing • swimming • have a picnic

Mr. Lopez

Marco

Mrs. Lopez

NATURAL HARDWOOD
LUMP
CHARCOAL

Unit Goals

Talk about past and future free-time activities

Write a letter about a vacation

Interpret information on a TV schedule

2 Listen

STUDENT TK 37
CLASS CD2 TK 38

A Listen. Write the letter of the conversation.

1. _____

2. _____

3. _____

4. _a_

5. _____

6. _____

STUDENT TK 37
CLASS CD2 TK 38

B Listen again to the conversations. Write the time word you hear.

A. I went hiking _____yesterday_____.

B. We went camping _____.

C. I was on vacation all _____.

D. Where were you _____?

E. I'm going to go swimming _____.

F. I went fishing _____.

Listen again. Check your answers.

3 After you listen

What do you do on your vacation? Check (✓) the boxes.

- ☐ go camping
- ☐ go fishing
- ☐ go hiking
- ☐ go swimming
- ☐ (other) _____

- ☐ go on a picnic
- ☐ relax / rest
- ☐ spend time with my family
- ☐ volunteer
- ☐ (other) _____

Talk with a partner. Ask and answer questions.

What do you do on your vacation?

I go hiking, swimming, and spend time with my family.

☑ Listen for and identify past and future free-time activities   **UNIT 10   123**

LESSON **B** What did you do yesterday?

1 **Grammar focus: simple past with irregular verbs**

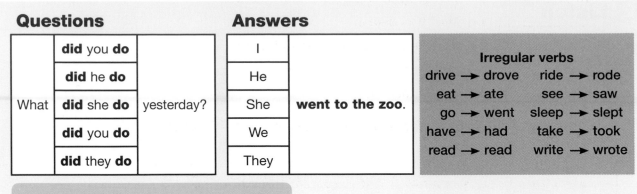

Questions		
	did you **do**	
	did he **do**	
What	**did** she **do**	yesterday?
	did you **do**	
	did they **do**	

Answers	
I	
He	
She	**went to the zoo**.
We	
They	

Irregular verbs

drive → drove   ride → rode
eat → ate   see → saw
go → went   sleep → slept
have → had   take → took
read → read   write → wrote

Turn to page 145 for a complete grammar chart.

2 **Practice**

A **Write.** Answer the questions.

1. **A** What did Carl and Gina do?
   B *They went to the zoo.*
   (go to the zoo)

2. **A** What did Paul do?
   B _____
   (take a driving test)

3. **A** What did Diane do?
   B _____
   (write a letter)

4. **A** What did Mrs. Nelson do?
   B _____
   (see the fireworks)

5. **A** What did Mr. Brown do?
   B _____
   (go fishing)

6. **A** What did Mr. and Mrs. Velez do?
   B _____
   (go dancing)

Listen and repeat. Then practice with a partner.

CLASS CD2 TK 39

B **Write.** Complete the sentences. Use the correct simple past form.

eat   go   have   ride   write

USEFUL LANGUAGE

Some activities follow
the word *go*:

go dancing

go fishing

go online

go shopping

go swimming

1. We ____*went*____ swimming in the pool last weekend.
2. I _____ my bike yesterday.
3. Silvia _____ e-mails to all her friends last week.
4. They _____ dinner very late last night.
5. We _____ a picnic last Sunday.

C **Talk** with a partner. Look at the schedule. Change the **bold** words and
make conversations.

Jeff Yu's Vacation Schedule

SUNDAY	MONDAY	TUESDAY	WEDNESDAY	THURSDAY	FRIDAY	SATURDAY
go to the museum	drive to the lake	ride my motorcycle	take swimming lessons	go hiking	have a picnic in the park	see a movie

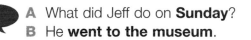

A What did Jeff do on **Sunday**?
B He **went to the museum**.

3 Communicate

Talk with three classmates. Complete the chart.

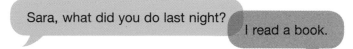

Sara, what did you do last night?

I read a book.

What did you do	Name	Name	Name
last night?			
yesterday morning?			
yesterday afternoon?			
the day before yesterday?			
last weekend?			

☑ Use the simple past of irregular verbs **UNIT 10** **125**

LESSON C What are you going to do?

1 Grammar focus: future with *be going to*

Questions				Answers				Time words
What	**are** you	**going to**	do tomorrow?	I**'m**	**going to**	take a trip.		today
	is he			He**'s**				tomorrow
	is she			She**'s**				tonight
	are they			They**'re**				next week
								next month

Turn to page 146 for a complete grammar chart.

2 Practice

A Write. Read the schedule. Answer the questions.

1. **A** What's Marta going to do next Monday?
   B She's _____ going to take a test _____.

2. **A** What's Paco going to do next Tuesday?
   B He's _____.

3. **A** What's Alfredo going to do next Wednesday?
   B He's _____.

4. **A** What are Mr. and Mrs. Santiago going to do next Thursday?
   B They're _____.

5. **A** What are Alfredo and Marta going to do next Friday?
   B They're _____.

6. **A** What's the family going to do next weekend?
   B They're _____.

Next Week's Schedule Santiago Family

Mon	Marta – take a test
Tues	Paco – play soccer
Wed	Alfredo – ride his bike
Thurs	Dad and Mom – go dancing
Fri	Alfredo and Marta – go to a party
Sat & Sun	The family – take a trip

Listen and repeat. Then practice with a partner.

CLASS CD2 TK 40

B **Talk** with a partner. Change the **bold** words and make conversations.

A What's **Brian** going to do today?
B **He's going to go to the beach.**
A That sounds like fun.

1. Brian / go to the beach
2. Ali / go shopping
3. Lisa / play soccer
4. Hiro and Lee / go fishing
5. Andrea / take a trip
6. Ray / go to a birthday party

3 Communicate

Talk to your classmates. Write their names and activities on the chart.

Yuri, what are you going to do next weekend?

I'm going to fix my car.

Name	Next weekend
Yuri	fix the car

☑ Use *be going to* for the future **UNIT 10** 127

LESSON D Reading

1 Before you read

Talk. Mrs. Lopez sent a picture of her family to a friend. Look at the picture. Answer the questions.

1. Who are the people in the picture?
2. What did they do?
3. What are they going to do next?

2 Read

Listen and read.

STUDENT TK 38
CLASS CD2 TK 41

New Message

From:	Maria
To:	Ming
Subject:	Hi

Dear Ming,

Last weekend, we went camping in the mountains. I went hiking. My husband and our sons went fishing. They also went swimming in the lake. We all had a great time!

Tonight we're going to eat fish for dinner. After dinner, we're going to watch a movie. Later tonight, we're going to be very busy. We are going to do the laundry. With three boys, we have a lot of dirty clothes!

See you soon,

Maria

> Look for words that show past or future time to help you understand.
> *Last weekend*
> *Tonight*

3 After you read

A Read the sentences. Are they correct? Circle *Yes* or *No*.

1. Last weekend, the Lopez family went shopping.   Yes   (No)
2. Mrs. Lopez went hiking.   Yes   No
3. Mr. Lopez and his wife went fishing.   Yes   No
4. The Lopez family is going to eat pizza for dinner.   Yes   No
5. After dinner, they are going to watch a movie.   Yes   No
6. They have a lot of clean clothes.   Yes   No

Write. Correct the sentences.

1. Last weekend, the Lopez family went <u>camping</u>.

B Write. Answer the questions about the Lopez family.

1. Who went fishing? _____
2. Who went swimming in the lake? _____
3. Is the Lopez family going to be busy tonight? _____

4 Picture dictionary Sports

1. _____*football*_____

2. _____

3. _____

4. _____

5. _____

6. _____

7. _____

8. _____

9. _____

A Write the words in the picture dictionary. Then listen and repeat.

STUDENT TK 30
CLASS CD2 TK 42

Use *play* with these words:

baseball	football	Ping-Pong
basketball	ice hockey	soccer

Use *go* with these words:

ice skating   skiing   surfing

B Talk with a partner. Look at the pictures and make conversations.

What's he going to do?

He's going to play football.

CULTURE NOTE

In the United States, football and soccer are different sports.

☑ Read an e-mail describing a vacation; use vocabulary for sports **UNIT 10 129**

LESSON E Writing

1 Before you write

A Talk with four classmates. Ask questions. Write the answers.

> **A** Where did you go on your last vacation?
> **B** I went to Arizona.
> **A** Who did you go with?
> **B** I went with my wife.
> **A** What did you do?
> **B** We visited the Grand Canyon.

Name	Where?	Who with?	Did what?
Omar	Arizona	wife	visited the Grand Canyon

B Read Maria's note. Answer the questions.

Maria

Dear Colleen,

I had a nice vacation. I went to Oregon. I went camping with my family. I read a book and rested. I went hiking. My husband and sons went fishing. We ate fish for dinner every night.

Next year, we are going to drive to New York. We are going to visit my mother and see the Statue of Liberty.

Did you have a nice vacation? What are you going to do on your next vacation?

See you soon,

Maria

1. Where did Maria go on vacation? _She went to Oregon._

2. What did Maria do? _____

3. What did her husband and sons do? _____

4. Where is Maria's family going next year? _____

5. What are they going to do? _____

2 Write

A Write. Answer the questions.

1. Where did you go on your last vacation?

   _____

   _____

2. Who did you go with?

   _____

   _____

3. What did you do?

   _____

   _____

a beach

4. Where are you going to go on your next vacation?

   _____

   _____

5. Who are you going to go with?

   _____

   _____

a zoo

6. What are you going to do?

   _____

   _____

B Write a letter about your vacations. Use the information from 2A.

> Begin a new paragraph when you change your ideas from the past to the future.

3 After you write

A Read your letter to a partner.

B Check your partner's letter.

- What are the past activities?
- What are the future activities?
- Are there different paragraphs for past and future activities?

LESSON F Another view

Saturday TV Schedule

	6:00	7:00	8:00	9:00
CHANNEL 7	Local news	Soccer		Swimming competition
CHANNEL 9	Cooking show	Boating program	*Great Places to Hike*	*Strange Animals*
CHANNEL 14	National news	Movie: *Camp Sunshine*		*Kids' Favorite Vacations*
CHANNEL 18	World news	*Fantastic Fishing*	Dancing competition	
CHANNEL 23	*Outdoor Adventures*	Baseball		

A Read the questions. Look at the TV schedule. Fill in the answer.

1. On what channel are they going to show a movie?

   Ⓐ on Channel 9

   Ⓑ on Channel 14

   Ⓒ on Channel 18

   Ⓓ on Channel 23

2. When is *Outdoor Adventures* going to be on?

   Ⓐ at 6:00 p.m.

   Ⓑ at 7:00 p.m.

   Ⓒ at 8:00 p.m.

   Ⓓ at 9:00 p.m

3. What are they going to show at 9 p.m. on Channel 9?

   Ⓐ *Great Places to Hike*

   Ⓑ *Kids' Favorite Vacations*

   Ⓒ *Fantastic Fishing*

   Ⓓ *Strange Animals*

4. How many channels are going to show the news at 6 p.m.?

   Ⓐ one channel

   Ⓑ two channels

   Ⓒ three channels

   Ⓓ five channels

B Talk with your classmates. Ask and answer the questions.

1. What did you watch on TV last night?
2. What are you going to watch on TV tomorrow night?
3. What are your favorite TV shows?
4. What do your family members watch on TV?

2 **Grammar connections:** past, present, and future

Simple past	Simple present	Future with *be going to*
Boris **went** to the movies last weekend.	Boris usually **cleans** his apartment on the weekends.	Boris **is going to go** hiking next weekend.

A Talk in a group. Complete the chart.

A What *did* you *do* last weekend, Boris?

B I *went* to the movies.

A What *do* you *do* every weekend?

B I usually *clean* my apartment.

A What *are* you *going to do* next weekend?

B I'*m going to go* hiking.

Name	Last weekend	Every weekend	Next weekend
Boris	went to the movies	cleans his apartment	is going to go hiking

B Share your group's information with the class.

A Boris went to the movies last weekend. He usually cleans his apartment every weekend. He's going to go hiking next weekend.

B Ling visited her sister last weekend. She usually . . .

3 **Wrap up**

Complete the **Self-assessment** on page 140.

Review

1 Listening

CLASS CD2 TK 43

Read the questions. Then listen and circle the answers.

1. When did Melissa's family go on a picnic?
   a. on Saturday
   b. on Sunday

2. What did they eat in the park?
   a. hot dogs
   b. hamburgers

3. When did Ivan's family do their chores?
   a. on Saturday
   b. on Sunday

4. Did Ivan wash the dishes?
   a. Yes, he did.
   b. No, he didn't.

5. What did Ivan's wife do?
   a. She washed the clothes.
   b. She vacuumed the rugs.

6. Who dusted the furniture?
   a. Tommy
   b. Lisa

Talk with a partner. Ask and answer the questions. Use complete sentences.

2 Grammar

A Write. Complete the story.

Two Weekends

Sam and Jenny _____*had*_____ a big party last weekend. On Saturday
                    1. have / had

morning, Jenny _____ the house and _____ dinner. Sam
               2. clean / cleaned   3. make / made

_____ the trash and _____ the patio.
4. empty / emptied   5. sweep / swept

   Next weekend, they're going to _____ to the mountains. Sam is
                                  6. drive / drove

going to _____ fishing. Jenny is going to _____ swimming
         7. go / went   8. go / went

in a lake.

B Write. Unscramble the words. Make questions about the story.

1. clean / When / Jenny / did / the house / ? ____*When did Jenny clean the house?*____

2. dinner / Sam / make / Did / ? _____

3. Sam / do / did / What / ? _____

4. next / do / going to / they / What / are / weekend / ?

   _____

Talk with a partner. Ask and answer the questions.

3 Pronunciation: the -ed ending in the simple past

A Listen to the -ed ending in these simple past verbs.

CLASS CD2 TK 44

/d/	/t/	/ɪd/
cleaned He cleaned his house.	cooked They cooked dinner.	dusted I dusted the living room.
dried I dried all the dishes.	talked She talked on the phone.	folded He folded his clothes.
emptied They emptied the trash.	washed She washed the car.	painted They painted the house.

B Listen and repeat.

CLASS CD2 TK 45

/d/	/t/	/ɪd/
exercised	camped	celebrated
played	fished	folded
turned	walked	visited

C Listen and check (✓) the correct column.

CLASS CD2 TK 46

	/d/	/t/	/ɪd/		/d/	/t/	/ɪd/
1. studied	✓			5. waited			
2. ironed				6. hiked			
3. mopped				7. vacuumed			
4. rested				8. worked			

Talk with a partner. Take turns. Make a sentence with each verb.

D Talk with a partner. Ask and answer the questions. Use correct pronunciation.

1. What did you do last weekend?   2. What did you do yesterday?

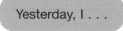

Last weekend, I . . .

Yesterday, I . . .

Self-assessments

UNIT 1 Personal information

A Vocabulary Check (✓) the words you know.

☐ address	✓ city	✓ last name	✓ street
✓ apartment number	✓ country	☐ middle name	✓ telephone number
✓ area code	✓ first name	✓ state	☐ zip code

B Skills and functions Read the sentences. Check (✓) what you know.

I can use possessive adjectives: *What's your* name? *My* name is _____.		I can read addresses with three or four numbers.	
I can use subject pronouns: *Is she from _____? Yes, she is. No, she isn't.*		I can complete a form with my personal information.	
I can begin names of people and places with capital letters.			

C What's next? Choose one.

☐ I am ready for the unit test.　　☐ I need more practice with _____.

UNIT 2 At school

A Vocabulary Check (✓) the words you know.

☐ calculator	☐ dictionary	☐ index cards	☐ notebook	☐ shelf
☐ calendar	☐ drawer	☐ map	☐ ruler	☐ stapler
☐ desk	☐ eraser	☐ marker	☐ scissors	☐ whiteboard

B Skills and functions Read the sentences. Check (✓) what you know.

I can use the prepositions *in*, *on*, and *under*: It's *on* the _____. It's *in* the _____. It's *under* the _____.		I can read and understand an inventory list.	
I can use singular and plural nouns: *The pen is on the desk. The pencils are on the table.*		I can start sentences with a capital letter and end them with a period.	
I can use *this / that* and *these / those*: *That's my pen. Those are my pencils.*		I can say *excuse me* to get someone's attention.	
I can look at a picture to help understand new words.			

C What's next? Choose one.

☐ I am ready for the unit test.　　☐ I need more practice with _____.

UNIT ③ Friends and family

✓ Assessment

A Vocabulary Check (✓) the words you know.

- ☐ aunt
- ☐ brother
- ☐ cousin
- ☐ daughter
- ☐ father
- ☐ grandfather
- ☐ grandmother
- ☐ husband
- ☐ mother
- ☐ nephew
- ☐ niece
- ☐ sister
- ☐ son
- ☐ uncle
- ☐ wife

B Skills and functions Read the sentences. Check (✓) what you know.

I can use the present continuous: **I am studying**.		I can use the title to understand a story.	
I can ask *yes / no* questions about the present: **Are** you **eating**?		I can spell the numbers from one to ten.	
I can use object pronouns: *She likes **it**. I like **him**.*		I can read a form with personal information on it.	
I can identify family members.			

C What's next? Choose one.

☐ I am ready for the unit test.   ☐ I need more practice with _____.

UNIT 4 Health

A Vocabulary Check (✓) the words you know.

- ☐ backache
- ☐ broken leg
- ☐ cold
- ☐ cough
- ☐ cut
- ☐ earache
- ☐ fever
- ☐ headache
- ☐ medicine
- ☐ sore throat
- ☐ sprained ankle
- ☐ stomachache

B Skills and functions Read the sentences. Check (✓) what you know.

I can use the simple present of **have**: *I **have** a headache. He **has** a cold.*		I can look for exclamation points when reading.	
I can ask questions with **have**: **Do** you **have** a headache?		I can write an excuse note about a sick child.	
I can use the simple present of **need**: *I **need** some aspirin.*		I can read an appointment card.	
I can write dates correctly.			

C What's next? Choose one.

☐ I am ready for the unit test.   ☐ I need more practice with _____.

UNIT 5 Around town

A **Vocabulary** Check (✓) the words you know.

- ☐ bank
- ☐ bus stop
- ☐ coffee shop
- ☐ grocery store
- ☐ hospital
- ☐ library
- ☐ pharmacy
- ☐ playground
- ☐ post office
- ☐ restaurant
- ☐ shopping mall
- ☐ train station

B **Skills and functions** Read the sentences. Check (✓) what you know.

I can use the prepositions **on**, **next to**, **across from**, **between**, and **on the corner of**.		I can give someone directions to places.	
I can use imperatives: **Turn** right. **Go** straight two blocks.		I can understand the pronouns (**I**, **he**, **it**, **they**) in a paragraph.	
I can use negative imperatives: **Don't turn** left. **Don't use** your cell phone here.		I can capitalize street names.	
I can read a map.			

C **What's next?** Choose one.

☐ I am ready for the unit test.   ☐ I need more practice with _____.

UNIT 6 Time

A **Vocabulary** Check (✓) the words you know.

- ☐ buy
- ☐ drink
- ☐ eat
- ☐ exercise
- ☐ get dressed
- ☐ get up
- ☐ pay bills
- ☐ play soccer
- ☐ read
- ☐ study
- ☐ take a break
- ☐ take a nap
- ☐ talk
- ☐ watch TV
- ☐ work

B **Skills and functions** Read the sentences. Check (✓) what you know.

I can use **at**, **in**, and **on** with time: *The meeting is **in** March. It is **on** Monday. It is **at** 1:00.*		I can ask questions to understand what I read: *Who, what, where, when?*	
I can ask **Wh-** questions about the present: **What** does he do in the evening?		I can indent when starting a paragraph.	
I can use **start** / **end** for events and **open** / **close** for places: *The meeting **ends** at 6 p.m. The building **closes** at 7 p.m.*		I can read a class schedule.	
I can talk about daily activities: *I eat dinner in the evening.*			

C **What's next?** Choose one.

☐ I am ready for the unit test.   ☐ I need more practice with _____.

UNIT 7 Shopping

A **Vocabulary** Check (✓) the words you know.

☐ apples	☐ check	☐ dime	☐ one-dollar bill	☐ shopping cart
☐ bananas	☐ cheese	☐ milk	☐ penny	☐ stock clerk
☐ cashier	☐ credit card	☐ nickel	☐ quarter	☐ water

B **Skills and functions** Read the sentences. Check (✓) what you know.

I can ask questions using *How many* and *How much*: *How many* eggs do we have? *How much* coffee do we have?		I can identify U.S. money.	
I can make sentences using *There is* and *There are*: *There is* rice on the shelf. *There are* two boxes of tea on the shelf.		I can use commas when listing three or more items.	
I can use *some* and *any*: We need *some* milk. We don't need *any* bread.		I can read a shopping ad.	
I can find clues to understand new words.			

C **What's next?** Choose one.

☐ I am ready for the unit test.   ☐ I need more practice with _____.

UNIT 8 Work

A **Vocabulary** Check (✓) the words you know.

☐ busperson	☐ homemaker	☐ nursing assistant	☐ salesperson
☐ construction worker	☐ housekeeper	☐ office worker	☐ server
☐ electrician	☐ nurse	☐ receptionist	☐ truck driver

B **Skills and functions** Read the sentences. Check (✓) what you know.

I can use the simple past of *be*: *Were* you a student? Yes, I *was*. No, I *wasn't*.		I can understand past and present when I read.	
I can use *can*: He *can* cook. She *can't* drive a truck.		I can use a dictionary to check my spelling.	
I can use *and* and *but* with *be*: John *is* at work today, *and* he *was* at work yesterday. Carmen *is* at work today, *but* she *wasn't* at work yesterday.		I can complete an employment application.	
I can write about my skills.			

C **What's next?** Choose one.

☐ I am ready for the unit test.   ☐ I need more practice with _____.

UNIT 9 Daily living

A Vocabulary Check (✓) the words you know.

- ☐ broom
- ☐ bucket
- ☐ clean
- ☐ dry
- ☐ dust
- ☐ dustpan
- ☐ empty
- ☐ iron
- ☐ lawn mower
- ☐ mop
- ☐ paint
- ☐ sponge
- ☐ sweep
- ☐ vacuum
- ☐ wash

B Skills and functions Read the sentences. Check (✓) what you know.

I can use the simple past with regular verbs: *They **mopped** yesterday. They **didn't vacuum**.*		I can read a note about daily chores.	
I can use the simple past with irregular verbs: *She **paid** the bills. He **didn't make** dinner.*		I can write a note about chores.	
I can ask and answer **or** questions: *Does Juan usually wash **or** sweep the floor? He usually sweeps the floor.*		I can check my simple past verb forms when writing.	
I can ask questions about what I am reading.		I can read a job-duties chart.	

C What's next? Choose one.

☐ I am ready for the unit test.   ☐ I need more practice with _____.

UNIT 10 Free time

A Vocabulary Check (✓) the words you know.

- ☐ baseball
- ☐ basketball
- ☐ camping
- ☐ fishing
- ☐ football
- ☐ have a picnic
- ☐ hiking
- ☐ ice skating
- ☐ museum
- ☐ skiing
- ☐ soccer
- ☐ surfing
- ☐ swimming
- ☐ vacation
- ☐ zoo

B Skills and functions Read the sentences. Check (✓) what you know.

I can talk about the past using irregular verbs: *What **did** you **do** last weekend? I **went** to the park.*		When I read, I can look for words that show past or future time.	
I can talk about the future using **be going to**: *I **am going to** play soccer tomorrow.*		I can begin a new paragraph when changing from the past to the future.	
I can ask and answer questions about the past, present, and future.		I can write about past and future vacations.	
I can read a letter about a person's vacation.		I can read a TV schedule.	

C What's next? Choose one.

☐ I am ready for the unit test.   ☐ I need more practice with _____.

Present of *be*

nalia.

you aren't.
I'm not.
he isn't.
she isn't.
it isn't.
you aren't.
we aren't.
they aren't.

Susan is eating dinner.

Present continuous

Affirmative statements

I'm	
You're	
He's	
She's	eating.
It's	
We're	
You're	
They're	

Yes / No questions

Am	I	
Are	you	
Is	he	
Is	she	eating?
Is	it	
Are	we	
Are	you	
Are	they	

Short answers

	you are.		you aren't.
	I am.		I'm not.
	he is.		he isn't.
Yes,	she is.	No,	she isn't.
	it is.		it isn't.
	you are.		you aren't.
	we are.		we aren't.
	they are.		they aren't.

Wh- questions

	am	I	
	are	you	
	is	he	
	is	she	
What	is	it	doing?
	are	we	
	are	you	
	are	they	

Answers

You're	
I'm	
He's	
She's	
It's	eating.
You're	
We're	
They're	

Possessive adjectives

Questions

	my	
	your	
	his	
What's	her	address?
	its	
	our	
	your	
	their	

Answers

Your	
My	
His	
Her	
Its	address is 10 Main Street.
Your	
Our	
Their	

Simple present

Affirmative statements

I	work.
You	work.
He	works.
She	works.
It	works.
We	work.
You	work.
They	work.

Negative statements

I	don't	
You	don't	
He	doesn't	
She	doesn't	work.
It	doesn't	
We	don't	
You	don't	
They	don't	

Yes / No questions

Do	I	
Do	you	
Does	he	
Does	she	work?
Does	it	
Do	we	
Do	you	
Do	they	

Short answers

	you	do.
	I	do.
	he	does.
Yes,	she	does.
	it	does.
	you	do.
	we	do.
	they	do.

	you	don't.
	I	don't.
	he	doesn't.
No,	she	doesn't.
	it	doesn't.
	you	don't.
	we	don't.
	they	don't.

Wh- questions: What

	do	I	
	do	you	
	does	he	
What	does	she	do at 7:00?
	does	it	
	do	we	
	do	you	
	do	they	

Answers

You	work.
I	work.
He	works.
She	works.
It	works.
You	work.
We	work.
They	work.

Wh- questions: When

	do	I	
	do	you	
	does	he	
When	does	she	usually work?
	does	it	
	do	we	
	do	you	
	do	they	

Answers

You	usually	work	
I			
He			
She	usually	works	
It			on Friday.
You			
We	usually	work	
They			

Simple present of have

Affirmative statements

I	have	
You	have	a cold.
He	has	
She	has	
We	have	
You	have	colds.
They	have	

Negative statements

I	don't have	
You	don't have	a cold.
He	doesn't have	
She	doesn't have	
We	don't have	
You	don't have	colds.
They	don't have	

Yes / No questions

Do	I	have	
Do	you	have	a cold?
Does	he	have	
Does	she	have	
Do	we	have	
Do	you	have	colds?
Do	they	have	

Short answers

	you	do.
	I	do.
	he	does.
Yes,	she	does.
	you	do.
	we	do.
	they	do.

	you	don't.
	I	don't.
	he	doesn't.
No,	she	doesn't.
	you	don't.
	we	don't.
	they	don't.

Simple past of be

Affirmative statements

I	was	
You	were	a teacher.
He	was	
She	was	
We	were	
You	were	teachers.
They	were	

Negative statements

I	wasn't	
You	weren't	a cashier.
He	wasn't	
She	wasn't	
We	weren't	
You	weren't	cashiers.
They	weren't	

Yes / No questions

Was	I	
Were	you	a teacher?
Was	he	
Was	she	
Were	we	
Were	you	teachers?
Were	they	

Short answers

	you	were.
	I	was.
	he	was.
Yes,	she	was.
	you	were.
	we	were.
	they	were.

	you	weren't.
	I	wasn't.
	he	wasn't.
No,	she	wasn't.
	you	weren't.
	we	weren't.
	they	weren't.

Simple past of regular and irregular verbs

Affirmative statements

I		I	
You		You	
He		He	
She	cooked.	She	slept.
It		It	
We		We	
You		You	
They		They	

Negative statements

I		
You		
He		
She	didn't	cook. / sleep.
It		
We		
You		
They		

Yes / No questions

	I	
	you	
	he	
	she	
Did	it	cook? / sleep?
	we	
	you	
	they	

Short answers

	you	
	I	
	he	
	she	
Yes,	it	did.
	you	
	we	
	they	

	you	
	I	
	he	
	she	
No,	it	didn't.
	you	
	we	
	they	

Wh- questions

		I		
		you		
		he		
		she		
What	did	it	do?	
		we		
		you		
		they		

Answers

You		You	
I		I	
He		He	
She	cooked.	She	slept.
It		It	
You		You	
We		We	
They		They	

Regular verbs

Add -ed: cook → cooked   vacuum → vacuumed
          dust → dusted   wash → washed

Irregular verbs

break → broke	get → got	ride → rode	sweep → swept
buy → bought	go → went	run → ran	swim → swam
do → did	have → had	see → saw	take → took
drink → drank	make → made	sell → sold	wear → wore
drive → drove	pay → paid	sit → sat	write → wrote
eat → ate	read → read	sleep → slept	

Can

Affirmative statements

I		
You		
He		
She	can	help.
It		
We		
You		
They		

Negative statements

I		
You		
He		
She	can't	help.
It		
We		
You		
They		

Yes / No questions

	I	
	you	
	he	
Can	she	help?
	it	
	we	
	you	
	they	

Short answers

	you	
	I	
	he	
Yes,	she	can.
	it	
	you	
	we	
	they	

	you	
	I	
	he	
No,	she	can't.
	it	
	you	
	we	
	they	

Future – *be going to*

Affirmative statements

I'm		
You're		
He's		
She's	going to	play soccer.
We're		
You're		
They're		

Negative statements

I'm		
You're		
He's		
She's	not going to	play soccer.
We're		
You're		
They're		

Wh- questions

	am	I	
	are	you	
	is	he	
What	is	she	going to do tomorrow?
	is	it	
	are	we	
	are	you	
	are	they	

Spelling rules

- Start sentences and names with capital letters:
  We live on Maple Street next to Mr. Smith.
- Write out numbers from one to ten:
  We have six cans of soda.
- Use numbers for values 11 and higher:
  We have 11 cans of soda.
- Verbs ending in *-y* take *-ied* in the simple past:
  dry → *dried*   *study* → *studied*
- Verbs ending in a vowel-consonant pair repeat the consonant in the simple past:
  mop → *mopped*

Punctuation rules

- Sentences can end with a period (.), question mark (?), or exclamation point (!):
  Simple statement: *We have coffee.*
  Question: *Do we have coffee?*
  Strong feeling: *We have coffee!*
- Put a comma after every item but the last when a list has three or more items:
  We have soda, coffee, and water.
- Begin paragraphs with an indent (space).
- Begin a new paragraph when you start a new topic or change the tense (time).

Capitalization rules

Begin the names of holidays with a capital letter.	**T**hanksgiving **L**abor **D**ay
Use capital letters for initials in a name.	Rafael **A.** Gomez **J. D.** Avona
Begin the opening and closing in a letter with a capital letter.	**D**ear Mrs. Jackson, **S**incerely, Maria Martinez
Use capital letters for acronyms.	**DMV** (**D**epartment of **M**otor **V**ehicles) **PTA** (**P**arent **T**eacher **A**ssociation)
Begin the names of classes with a capital letter.	**B**usiness **E**nglish **I**ntroduction to **C**omputers
Begin the names of languages with a capital letter.	**V**ietnamese **E**nglish
Begin the names of TV shows and movies with a capital letter.	**S**trange **A**nimals **C**amp **S**unshine
Begin abbreviations for days of the week with a capital.	**M**on. **S**at.

Cardinal numbers

0 zero	10 ten	20 twenty	30 thirty	40 forty
1 one	11 eleven	21 twenty-one	31 thirty-one	50 fifty
2 two	12 twelve	22 twenty-two	32 thirty-two	60 sixty
3 three	13 thirteen	23 twenty-three	33 thirty-three	70 seventy
4 four	14 fourteen	24 twenty-four	34 thirty-four	80 eighty
5 five	15 fifteen	25 twenty-five	35 thirty-five	90 ninety
6 six	16 sixteen	26 twenty-six	36 thirty-six	100 one hundred
7 seven	17 seventeen	27 twenty-seven	37 thirty-seven	1,000 one thousand
8 eight	18 eighteen	28 twenty-eight	38 thirty-eight	
9 nine	19 nineteen	29 twenty-nine	39 thirty-nine	

Ordinal numbers

1st first	11th eleventh	21st twenty-first	31st thirty-first
2nd second	12th twelfth	22nd twenty-second	
3rd third	13th thirteenth	23rd twenty-third	
4th fourth	14th fourteenth	24th twenty-fourth	
5th fifth	15th fifteenth	25th twenty-fifth	
6th sixth	16th sixteenth	26th twenty-sixth	
7th seventh	17th seventeenth	27th twenty-seventh	
8th eighth	18th eighteenth	28th twenty-eighth	
9th ninth	19th nineteenth	29th twenty-ninth	
10th tenth	20th twentieth	30th thirtieth	

Metric equivalents

1 inch = 25 millimeters	1 dry ounce = 28 grams	1 fluid ounce = 30 milliliters
1 foot = 30 centimeters	1 pound = .45 kilograms	1 quart = .95 liters
1 yard = .9 meters	1 mile = 1.6 kilometers	1 gallon = 3.8 liters

Converting Fahrenheit temperatures to Celsius

Subtract 30 and divide by 2.
Example: 80°F − 30 = 50; 50 divided by 2 = 25
80°F = approximately 25°C

Countries and nationalities

Country	Nationality	Country	Nationality	Country	Nationality
Afghanistan	Afghan	Germany	German	Portugal	Portuguese
Albania	Albanian	Ghana	Ghanaian	Puerto Rico	Puerto Rican
Algeria	Algerian	Greece	Greek	Republic of the Congo	Congolese
Angola	Angolan	Grenada	Grenadian	Romania	Romanian
Argentina	Argentine	Guatemala	Guatemalan	Russia	Russian
Armenia	Armenian	Guyana	Guyanese	Saudi Arabia	Saudi
Australia	Australian	Haiti	Haitian	Senegal	Senegalese
Austria	Austrian	Herzegovina	Herzegovinian	Serbia	Serbian
Azerbaijan	Azerbaijani	Honduras	Honduran	Sierra Leone	Sierra Leonean
Bahamas	Bahamian	Hungary	Hungarian	Singapore	Singaporean
Bahrain	Bahraini	India	Indian	Slovakia	Slovak
Bangladesh	Bangladeshi	Indonesia	Indonesian	Somalia	Somali
Barbados	Barbadian	Iran	Iranian	South Africa	South African
Belarus	Belarusian	Iraq	Iraqi	South Korea	Korean
Belgium	Belgian	Ireland	Irish	Spain	Spanish
Belize	Belizean	Israel	Israeli	Sri Lanka	Sri Lankan
Benin	Beninese	Italy	Italian	Sudan	Sudanese
Bolivia	Bolivian	Jamaica	Jamaican	Sweden	Swedish
Bosnia	Bosnian	Japan	Japanese	Switzerland	Swiss
Brazil	Brazilian	Jordan	Jordanian	Syria	Syrian
Bulgaria	Bulgarian	Kazakhstan	Kazakhstani	Tajikistan	Tajikistani
Cambodia	Cambodian	Kenya	Kenyan	Tanzania	Tanzanian
Cameroon	Cameroonian	Kuwait	Kuwaiti	Thailand	Thai
Canada	Canadian	Laos	Laotian	Togo	Togolese
Cape Verde	Cape Verdean	Lebanon	Lebanese	Tonga	Tongan
Chile	Chilean	Liberia	Liberian	Trinidad	Trinidadian
China	Chinese	Lithuania	Lithuanian	Tunisia	Tunisian
Colombia	Colombian	Macedonia	Macedonian	Turkey	Turkish
Comoros	Comoran	Malaysia	Malaysian	Turkmenistan	Turkmen
Costa Rica	Costa Rican	Mexico	Mexican	Uganda	Ugandan
Côte d'Ivoire	Ivoirian	Morocco	Moroccan	Ukraine	Ukrainian
Croatia	Croatian	Myanmar (Burma)	Myanmar (Burmese)	United Arab Emirates	Emirati
Cuba	Cuban	Nepal	Nepali	United Kingdom	British
Dominica	Dominican	Netherlands	Dutch	United States	American
Dominican Republic	Dominican	New Zealand	New Zealander	Uruguay	Uruguayan
Ecuador	Ecuadorian	Nicaragua	Nicaraguan	Uzbekistan	Uzbekistani
Egypt	Egyptian	Niger	Nigerien	Venezuela	Venezuelan
El Salvador	Salvadoran	Nigeria	Nigerian	Vietnam	Vietnamese
Equatorial Guinea	Equatorial Guinean	Norway	Norwegian	Yemen	Yemeni
Eritrea	Eritrean	Pakistan	Pakistani	Zambia	Zambian
Ethiopia	Ethiopian	Panama	Panamanian	Zimbabwe	Zimbabwean
Fiji	Fijian	Paraguay	Paraguayan		
France	French	Peru	Peruvian		
Georgia	Georgian	Philippines	Filipino		
		Poland	Polish		

Map of North America

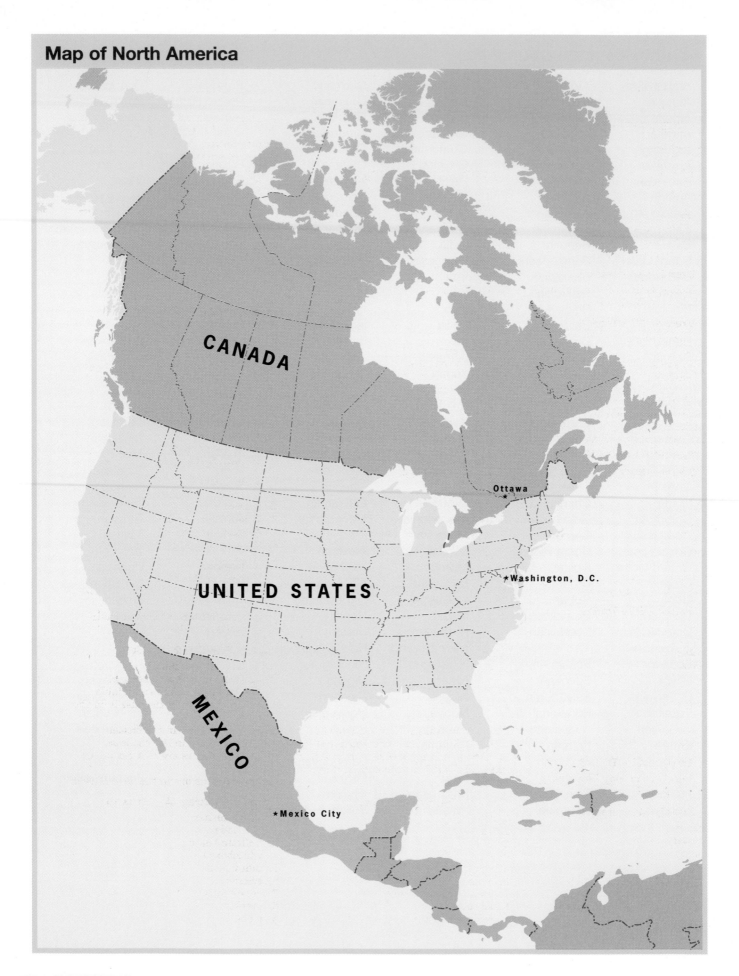

CANADA

UNITED STATES

★ Ottawa

★ Washington, D.C.

MEXICO

★ Mexico City

Self-study audio script

Welcome

Page 3, Exercise 2A – Track 2

Conversation A
A Hi, I'm Paolo. What's your name?
B I'm Ryoko.
A How do you spell that?
B R-Y-O-K-O.

Conversation B
A Hi, Kankou. How's it going?
   This is my friend Eduardo.
B Nice to meet you, Eduardo.

Page 3, Exercise 2B – Track 3

A, B, C, D, E, F, G, H, I, J, K, L, M, N, O,
P, Q, R, S, T, U, V, W, X, Y, Z

Page 3, Exercise 2C – Track 4

A What's your name?
B Helena.
A How do you spell that?
B H-E-L-E-N-A.

Page 4, Exercise 3A – Track 5

Zero, one, two, three, four, five, six,
seven, eight, nine, ten, eleven, twelve,
thirteen, fourteen, fifteen, sixteen,
seventeen, eighteen, nineteen, twenty

Page 4, Exercise 3B – Track 6

1. six
2. twenty
3. one
4. fifteen
5. nine
6. twelve
7. eight
8. five
9. sixteen

Page 4, Exercise 3C – Track 7

1. three
2. eight
3. eighteen
4. twelve
5. one
6. zero
7. twenty
8. four
9. fifteen
10. eleven

Page 5, Exercise 4A – Track 8

Sunday, Monday, Tuesday, Wednesday,
Thursday, Friday, Saturday

Page 5, Exercise 4C – Track 9

1. January
2. February
3. March
4. April
5. May
6. June
7. July
8. August
9. September
10. October
11. November
12. December

Unit 1: Personal information

Page 7, Exercises 2A and 2B – Track 10

Conversation A
A What's your telephone number?
B My telephone number is 555-8907.
A Was that 555-8807?
B No, it's 555-8907.

Conversation B
A What's your area code?
B My area code?
A Yes.
B It's 213.
A 213. OK, thanks.

Conversation C
A What's your last name?
B Clark. Mister Clark.
A Clark? Please spell that.
B C-L-A-R-K.
A Thank you.

Conversation D
A What's your address?
B 1041 Main Street.
A 1014 Main Street?
B No, 1041.
A OK. Thank you.

Conversation E
A What's your first name?
B Ricardo.
A R-I-K-A . . .
B No, R-I-C-A-R-D-O.
A OK, R-I-C-A-R-D-O. Thanks.

Conversation F
A What's your zip code?
B 94558.
A Is that 94458?
B No, 94558.
A OK. Thanks.

Page 12, Exercise 2 – Track 11

A New Student
    Svetlana Kulik is a new student.
She is from Russia. Now she lives in
Napa, California. Her address is 1041
Main Street. Her zip code is 94558. Her
area code is 707. Her telephone number
is 555-9073.

Page 13, Exercise 4A – Track 12

1. title
2. address
3. city
4. state
5. signature
6. zip code
7. apartment number
8. street
9. middle initial

Unit 2: At school

Page 19, Exercises 2A and 2B – Track 13

Conversation A
A Where are the pens?
B The pins?
A No, the pens.
B Oh, they're in the drawer.
A Thanks.

Conversation B
A Where's the calculator?
B The what?
A The calculator.
B Oh. Look in the desk.
A Thank you.

Conversation C
A Where's the notebook?
B The notebook?
A Yes.
B I see it on the table.
A Oh, good.

Conversation D
A Erika, where's the stapler?
B The what?
A The stapler.
B It's in the drawer.
A Thanks, Erika.

Conversation E
A Where are the rulers?
B Excuse me?
A Where are the rulers?
B Are they in the box?
A Oh, yes. Now I see them.

Conversation F
B Where's my book?
A Your book?
B Yeah.
A It's on the floor under your chair.
B Oh, good. Thanks.

Page 24, Exercise 2 – Track 14

Attention, new students!
Welcome to your new classroom.
• The laptop is on the small table.
• The pencils are in the basket on the
  desk.
• The erasers are in the basket.
• The books are in the bookcase.
• The calculators are in a box under
  the table.
• The markers are in the desk drawer.

Page 25, Exercise 4A – Track 15

1. hole puncher
2. notepads
3. bulletin board
4. whiteboard
5. index cards
6. scissors
7. paper clips
8. marker
9. globe

Unit 3: Friends and family

Page 33, Exercises 2A and 2B – Track 16

Conversation A
A Hello?
B Hi, Luisa. This is Mrs. Brown. Is your grandmother home?
A Yes, she is. She's watching TV.
B Can I talk to her?
A Sure, just a minute.

Conversation B
A Hello?
B Hi . . . Carlos? This is Mr. Cho. Is your father home?
A Yes, he is, but he's sleeping right now.
B Oh, I'm sorry. I can call again later.
A OK, thanks.

Conversation C
A Hello?
B Hi, Carlos. This is Mr. Ramos. Is your grandfather there?
A Yes, he is, but he's eating lunch right now.
B OK. I'll call him later.
A Thanks.

Conversation D
A Hello?
B Hi, this is Angela. Is your mother there?
A Yes, she is. But she's busy. She's cooking dinner.
B Oh, OK. I'll call back after dinner.
A OK, thanks.

Conversation E
A Hello?
B Hi, Carlos. This is Mary. Is your sister home?
A She's here, but she's studying.
B Oh, OK. Please ask her to call me later.
A Sure. No problem.

Conversation F
A Hello?
B Hello. Is this Mrs. Gonzalez?
A Yes, it is.
B This is Dr. Smith's office. Is your husband home?
A Yes, he is, but he's resting.
B Oh, OK. Please ask him to call our office.

Page 38, Exercise 2 – Track 17

The Birthday Party
My name is Juan. In this picture, it's my birthday. I am 70 years old. Look at me! I don't look 70 years old. My wife, my daughter, and my grandson are eating cake. My grandson is always hungry. My granddaughter is drinking soda. She's always thirsty. My son-in-law is playing the guitar and singing. Everyone is happy!

Page 39, Exercise 4A – Track 18

1. grandfather and grandmother
2. father and mother
3. aunt and uncle
4. brother and sister-in-law
5. husband and wife
6. cousin
7. niece and nephew

Unit 4: Health

Page 45, Exercises 2A and 2B – Track 19

Conversation A
A What's the matter? You aren't reading.
B No, I'm not.
A Why not?
B I have a headache.
A Oh, I'm sorry to hear that.

Conversation B
A Are you all right?
B No, not really. I have a fever.
A Get some rest. I hope you get well soon.
B Thank you. I'm sure I will.

Conversation C
A What's the matter?
B I have a sprained ankle.
A A sprained ankle? Try an ice pack.
B Thanks for the advice.
A I hope it gets better soon.
B Thanks. I'm sure it will.

Conversation D
A Are you OK?
B No, not really. I have a stomachache.
A A stomachache? That's too bad.
B Yes, a really bad stomachache.
A Well then, take it easy.
B Thanks. I will.

Conversation E
A You don't look well. What's wrong?
B I have a sore throat.
A Oh, I'm sorry. Get some rest.
B Thank you. I will.

Conversation F
A You don't look well. What's wrong?
B I have an earache.
A An earache, huh?
B Yeah.
A I'm sorry.

Page 50, Exercise 2 – Track 20

The Doctor's Office
Poor Maria! Everyone is sick! Maria and her children are in the doctor's office. Her son, Luis, has a sore throat. Her daughter, Rosa, has a stomachache. Her baby, Gabriel, has an earache. Maria doesn't have a sore throat. She doesn't have a stomachache. And she doesn't have an earache. But Maria has a very bad headache!

Page 51, Exercise 4A – Track 21

1. nose
2. teeth
3. finger
4. stomach
5. leg
6. hand
7. back
8. eye
9. toe
10. foot
11. knee
12. neck
13. ear
14. head
15. mouth
16. chin
17. shoulder

Unit 5: Around town

Page 59, Exercises 2A and 2B – Track 22

Conversation A
A Excuse me. Where's the pharmacy?
B The pharmacy? It's on 5th Avenue.
A 5th Avenue? Is it far from here?
B No, just go straight about two blocks.
A Thank you very much.

Conversation B
A Excuse me. I'm looking for the museum.
B The museum? Hmmm. Oh yes. It's on C Street.
A C Street? Where is that?
B It's not far. Turn left at the next street.
A Thanks a lot.

Conversation C
A Excuse me. I can't find the post office.
B The post office? It's on 70th Street.
A 70th Street? That way?
B Yes, just go that way a block.
A Thanks for your help.

Conversation D
A Excuse me. Is the bus stop around here?
B The bus stop? Let's see . . . yes, it's on G Street.
A G Street? Is that far?
B No, it's across the street.
A Thank you. I appreciate it.

Conversation E
A Excuse me. I'm looking for the playground.
B The playground? It's on First Avenue.
A First Avenue? Where is that?
B Go to the corner and turn left.
A Thanks so much.

Conversation F
A Excuse me. Is there a restaurant near here?
B A restaurant? Oh yes! It's on Third Avenue.
A Third Avenue? Over there?
B Yes, it's not far. Go straight a few more blocks. It's on your right.
A Great! Thanks a lot.

Page 64, Exercise 2 – Track 23

Hi Angela,

I love my new house. My neighborhood is great! Here are some pictures.

There is a school on my street. My children go to the school. They like it a lot. There is a community center across from the school. My husband works at the community center. He walks to work. There is a grocery store next to my house. It's a small store, but we can buy a lot of things. There is a good Mexican restaurant on Second Street. It's right across from my house.

I like it here, but I miss you. Please write.

Your friend,
Sandra

Page 65, Exercise 4A – Track 24

1. a shopping mall
2. a high school
3. a day-care center
4. a senior center
5. a playground
6. a police station
7. an apartment building
8. a hardware store
9. a courthouse

Unit 6: Time

Page 71, Exercises 2A and 2B – Track 25

Conversation A
A Congratulations on your new job.
B Thanks.
A So when do you leave for work?
B I leave at ten-thirty.
A At night?
B Right.

Conversation B
A What time do you eat dinner?
B We eat dinner at six-thirty.
A And you don't go to work until ten-thirty?
B That's right.

Conversation C
A What time do you start work?
B I start work at eleven o'clock at night.
A So it takes you half an hour to get there?
B Yeah.

Conversation D
A What time do you catch the bus?
B I catch the bus at ten forty-five.
A Ten forty-five? Not ten-thirty?
B Right. Ten forty-five, not ten-thirty.

Conversation E
A What time do you take a break?
B I take a break at two forty-five in the morning.
A Two forty-five? Wow. I'm sleeping then!
B I know. So is my family.

Conversation F
A What time do you get home?
B I get home around seven-thirty.
A In the morning?
B Right. Just in time for breakfast!

Page 76, Exercise 2 – Track 26

Meet Our New Employee: Bob Green
    Please welcome Bob. He is a new security guard. He works the night shift

at the East End Factory. Bob starts work at 11:00 at night. He leaves work at 7:00 in the morning.
    Bob likes these hours because he can spend time with his family. Bob says, "I eat breakfast with my wife, Arlene, and my son, Brett, at 7:30 every morning. I help Brett with his homework in the afternoon. I eat dinner with my family at 6:30. Then we watch TV. At 10:30, I go to work."
    Congratulations to Bob on his new job!

Page 77, Exercise 4A – Track 27

1. get up
2. eat breakfast
3. take a shower
4. get dressed
5. take the children to school
6. eat lunch
7. walk the dog
8. eat dinner
9. go to bed

Unit 7: Shopping

Page 85, Exercises 2A and 2B – Track 28

Conversation A
A We need some milk. Is there any milk on sale?
B Yes. Milk is two sixty-nine.
A Two sixty-nine? That's cheap.
B How much do we need?
A A lot.

Conversation B
A Let's get some onions. Are there any good onions?
B Here are the onions. They're seventy-nine cents each.
A Whoa! Seventy-nine cents each! That's expensive.
B How many do we need?
A We just need one.
B OK.

Conversation C
A Are there any tomatoes on sale? We need some tomatoes.
B Oh look! They're one twenty-nine a pound.
A Really? That's cheap.
B How many do we need?
A Let's get a lot.

Conversation D
A Do we need any cheese? I see cheese is just six ninety-nine a pound.
B Six ninety-nine? Hey! That's good.
A How much do we need?
B Not much. Let's get half a pound.

Conversation E
A We need some potatoes. Are there any potatoes on sale this week?
B Yes. Potatoes are ninety-nine cents a pound.
A Wow! That's a good price.
B How many do we need?
A A lot!

Conversation F
A Is there any bread on sale?
B No, bread is three seventy-nine.
A What? That's not very good.
B Well, how much do we need?
A Not much.

Page 90, Exercise 2 – Track 29

Regular Customers
    Shirley and Dan are regular customers at SaveMore Supermarket. They go to SaveMore three or four times a week. The cashiers and stock clerks at SaveMore know them and like them. There are fruit and vegetables, meat and fish, and cookies and cakes in the supermarket. But today, Shirley and Dan are buying apples, bananas, bread, and cheese. There is one problem. The total is $16.75. They only have a ten-dollar bill, 5 one-dollar bills, and three quarters!

Page 91, Exercise 4A – Track 30

1. a penny
2. a nickel
3. a dime
4. a quarter
5. a half-dollar
6. a one-dollar bill
7. a five-dollar bill
8. a ten-dollar bill
9. a twenty-dollar bill
10. a check
11. a credit card
12. a debit card

Unit 8: Work

Page 97, Exercises 2A and 2B – Track 31

Conversation A
A What does he do?
B He's a manager at a restaurant.
A Oh, really? What did he do before?
B He was a cashier.
A A cashier? When?
B For a while, I think from 1998 to 2010.

Conversation B
A What does Irene do?
B She's a nurse.
A Oh, that's nice. What did she do before?
B She was a cook.
A A cook? When?
B From 2011 to 2012.

Conversation C
A What does Brenda do?
B She's a teacher.
A Oh, that's great. What did she do before?
B She was a server.
A A server? When?
B Last year, from about May to August.

Conversation D
A What does he do?
B He's a busperson.
A Oh, really? What did he do before?
B He was a student.

A A student? When?
B For about six months, from January to June.

Conversation E
A What does he do?
B He's an electrician.
A Oh, yeah? What did he do before?
B He was a construction worker.
A A construction worker? When?
B I think it was in 2012.

Conversation F
A What does she do?
B She's a doctor.
A Oh, that's great. What did she do before?
B She was a medical student.
A A medical student? When?
B I'm not sure, but I think at least 15 years ago.

Page 102, Exercise 2 – Track 32
Dear Ms. Carter:

I am writing this letter to recommend my student Mai Linh Lam.
Mai Linh was a teacher in Vietnam. She is looking for a new job in the United States. She is a certified nursing assistant now. She volunteers in a nursing home Monday through Friday from 12:00 to 4:30. She takes care of senior citizens.
Mai Linh has many good skills. She can write reports. She can help elderly people move around and sit down. She can help them eat. She can also speak English and Vietnamese. These skills are useful in her job, and she is very good at her work.

Sincerely,
Elaine Maxwell

Page 103, Exercise 4A – Track 33
1. housekeeper
2. custodian
3. pharmacy technician
4. factory worker
5. hairstylist
6. dental assistant

Unit 9: Daily living
Page 111, Exercises 2A and 2B – Track 34

Conversation A
A Did you wash the clothes?
B No I didn't, but Rachel did.
A She did? When?
B She washed them last night.
A Good for her!

Conversation B
A Did you pay the bills?
B Yes, I did.
A Are you sure? When?
B I paid them yesterday morning.
A That's great! Thank you.

Conversation C
A Suzy, did you clean the bathroom?
B No, I didn't, but Rita did.

A Oh? When did she clean it?
B She cleaned it the day before yesterday.
A OK. Good.

Conversation D
A Frank, the rug is really clean. Did you vacuum it?
B Yes, I did.
A Did you do it last Friday?
B I vacuumed it every day last week.
A Every day? That's wonderful!

Conversation E
A Did Alice dust the bookshelves?
B Yes, she did.
A Oh, that's good.
B Yes, I told her yesterday.
A Well, I'll thank her.

Conversation F
A Ralph, did you mop the floor or did Victor do it?
B I mopped it.
A When?
B Last night.
A Well, it's dirty again!

Page 116, Exercise 2 – Track 35
Dear Karen,

Welcome home! We were very busy today. Jeff ironed the clothes. Chris emptied the trash. Sharon mopped the floor. Ben vacuumed the rug and dusted the furniture. The house is clean for you!
I cooked dinner. There is food on the stove.

Your husband,
Mark

Page 117, Exercise 4A – Track 36
1. a sponge
2. a mop
3. a vacuum cleaner
4. a dustpan
5. an iron
6. a broom
7. a stove
8. a lawn mower
9. a bucket

Unit 10: Free time
Page 123, Exercises 2A and 2B – Track 37

Conversation A
A Hi, Diego!
B Oh! Hi, Carla. How are you? You look tired.
A Oh, no, I'm OK. I went hiking yesterday.
B Really, where?
A We went up to Bear Mountain.
B That's great. I'm going to go hiking next weekend.

Conversation B
A Hi, Nicholas. How are you?
B Oh, pretty good. What's new with you?
A Well, we went camping last weekend.
B Really? Did you have fun?

A Yes. When are you going to go camping?
B We're going to go camping next week.

Conversation C
A Hey, Bill. How are you?
B Terrific. I was on vacation all last week.
A Really? What did you do?
B Nothing. I just relaxed all day. When are you going to take a vacation?
A I'm going to take my vacation next month.

Conversation D
A Hi, Shawn. Where were you last Sunday?
B I went with my family to Lookout Park. We went on a picnic.
A Really? I'm going to have a picnic there next weekend.
B Well, watch out for the bees!
A I will. Thanks for telling me about them.

Conversation E
A Lidia, where were you yesterday?
B It was pretty hot, so we went swimming at the lake.
A Really? I'm going to go swimming next weekend.
B Great. Where?
A In the pool at my school.
B Have fun!

Conversation F
A Hey, Barbara, where did you get those fish?
B I went fishing today.
A Where did you go?
B We went to Lake Jenner.
A That sounds like fun. I'm going to go fishing there tomorrow.
B Good luck.

Page 128, Exercise 2 – Track 38
Dear Ming,

Last weekend, we went camping in the mountains. I went hiking. My husband and our sons went fishing. They also went swimming in the lake. We all had a great time!

Tonight we're going to eat fish for dinner. After dinner, we're going to watch a movie. Later tonight, we're going to be very busy. We are going to do the laundry. With three boys, we have a lot of dirty clothes!

See you soon,

Maria

Page 129, Exercise 4A – Track 39
1. football
2. baseball
3. basketball
4. Ping-Pong
5. ice hockey
6. soccer
7. surfing
8. ice skating
9. skiing

Illustration credits

Kenneth Batelman: 89
Cybele: 37 (t), 87
Travis Foster: 78
Chuck Gonzales: 29 (b), 35, 48, 112, 113
Stuart Holmes: 26, 68
Jim Kopp: 25 (#2, 3, 5, 7, 8, 9), 66, 77

Frank Montagna: 11, 40, 51 (t), 124
Greg Paprocki: 21, 107, 127
Q2A Media Services: 2, 17, 19, 20 (b), 24, 25 (#1, 4, 6), 29 (t), 36, 37 (b), 38, 39, 43, 55, 69, 74, 95, 105, 121, 133
Maria Rabinky: 60 (b), 61 (t), 63
Lucie Rice: 100
Monika Roe: 22, 23, 27, 73, 92, 114

Photography credits

Cover front (tl) Andrew Zarivny/Shutterstock, (tr) Stuart Monk/Shutterstock, (r) Gary D Ercole/Photolibrary/Getty Images, (cr) Sam Kolich; (br) Nathan Maxfield/iStockphoto, (c) Monkey Business Images/Shutterstock, (bl) Alistair Forrester Shankie/iStockphoto, (cl) ML Harris/Iconica/Getty Images, (l) Mark Lewis/Digital Vision/Getty Images, back (tc) cloki/Shutterstock, (br) gualtiero boffi/Shutterstock, **4** (br) ©Chris Schmidt/iStockphoto, **5** (bl) ©Izabela Habur/iStockphoto, **8** (tcr) ©Valua Vitaly/Shutterstock, (tl) ©Andres Rodriguez/Fotolia, (tc) ©iofoto/Shutterstock, (tr) ©Blend Images/Shutterstock, (bl) ©michael spring/Fotolia, (bc) ©WONG SZE FEI/Fotolia, (br) ©Image Source IS2/Fotolia, **9** (tr) ©michaeljung/Shutterstock, **13** (tl) ©fotoluminate/Shutterstock, **15** (tr) ©Monart Design/Fotolia, **19** (tl) ©WitthayaP/Shutterstock, (tc) ©DLeonis/Fotolia, (tr) ©MTrebbin/Shutterstock, (bl) ©Virunja/Shutterstock, (bc) ©hadahos/Fotolia, (br) ©alekc79/Fotolia, **22** (tl) ©Julia Ivantsova/Shutterstock, (bl) ©Melinda Fawver/Shutterstock, (tc) ©Alex Staroseltsev/Shutterstock, (bc) ©Michal Modzelewski/Shutterstock, (tr) ©MTrebbin/Shutterstock, (br) ©studioVin/Shutterstock, **34** (tl) ©Jane norton/iStockphoto, (tc) ©Pearl Jackson/iStockphoto, (tr) ©Jupiterimages/Getty Images, (bl) ©George Blonsky/Alamy, (bc) ©Stokkete/Shutterstock, (br) ©zhu difeng/Shutterstock, **35** (bcr) ©PhotosIndia.com LLC/Alamy, (br) ©Luis Santos/Shutterstock, **45** (tl) ©Kay Blaschke/Getty Images, (tc) ©Yuri Arcurs/Fotolia, (tr) ©Robert Kneschke/Fotolia, (bl) ©Bubbles Photolibrary/Alamy, (bc) ©Custom Medical Stock Photo/Alamy, (br) ©Image Source/Alamy, **46** (tl) ©iceteastock/Fotolia, (tc) ©Robert Kneschke/Fotolia, (tr) ©Monkey Business Images/Shutterstock, (l) ©Blend Images/Alamy, (c) ©Julija Sapic/Fotolia, (r) ©Tom Le Goff/Thinkstock, (bl) ©konzeptm/Fotolia, (bc) ©Monkey Business/Fotolia, (br) ©Image Source/Alamy, **47** (tl) ©Cameramannz/Shutterstock, (tc) ©James Steidl/Shutterstock, (tr) ©Svetlana Lukienko/Shutterstock, (bl) ©Helen Sessions/Alamy, (bc) ©Jim Barber/Fotolia, (br) ©imagebroker/Alamy, **49** (tl) ©Monkey Business Images/Shutterstock, (tc) ©wavebreakmedia/Shutterstock, (tr) ©richardlyons/Fotolia, (bl) ©baki/Shutterstock, (bc) ©Chris Fertnig/iStockphoto, (br) ©Gabriel Blaj/Fotolia, **59** (tl) ©JoeFox/Alamy, (tc) ©david hughes/Fotolia, (tr) ©Graham Oliver/Alamy, (bl) ©Robert Convery/Alamy, (bc) ©incamerastock/Alamy, (br) ©Jim West/Alamy, **65** (tl) ©Chuck Pefley/Alamy, (tc) ©Jamie Pham/Alamy, (cl) ©Yvan Dube/Getty Images, (c) ©StockLite/Shutterstock, (cr) ©Christine Glade/iStockphoto, (bl) ©Konstantin L/Shutterstock, (bc) ©Stockbyte/Thinkstock, (br) ©Steve Heap/Shutterstock, (tr) ©matka_Wariatka/Shutterstock, **69** (tl) ©Carlos Santa Maria/Fotolia, (tc) ©yobidaba/Fotolia, (tr) ©Hung Chung Chih/Shutterstock, (bl) ©Stephen Finn/Shutterstock, (bc) ©Arcady/Shutterstock, (br) ©Georgios Kollidas/Shutterstock, **72** (tl) ©WavebreakMediaMicro/Fotolia, (tr) ©Blend Images/Alamy, (bl) ©Juice Images/Alamy, (br) ©ZINQ Stock/Fotolia, **85** (tl) ©iStockphoto/Thinkstock, (tc) ©Chris Curtis/Shutterstock, (tr) ©vlorzor/Fotolia, (bl) ©EuToch/Fotolia, (bc) ©Stockbyte/Thinkstock, (br) ©iStockphoto/Thinkstock, **86** (tl) ©Orlando Bellini/Fotolia, (tcl) ©Maksym Protsenko/Fotolia, (tcr) ©lubashi/Fotolia, (tr) ©M.studio/Fotolia, (l) ©slon1971/Shutterstock, (cl) ©Ian 2010/Fotolia, (cr) ©antpkr/Fotolia, (r) ©stockcreations/Fotolia, (bl) ©piotr_pabijan/Shutterstock, (bcl) ©Valery121283/Shutterstock, (bcr) ©velesdesign/Fotolia, (br) ©Peter Zijlstra/Shutterstock, **91** (penny) rsooll/Fotolia, (nickel) rsooll/Fotolia, (dime) mattesimages/Fotolia, (quarter) jackmicro/Fotolia, (half dollar) mattesimages/Shutterstock, (dollar) jaanall/Fotolia, (five dollar) schankz/Fotolia, (ten dollar) acilo/iStockphoto, (twenty dollar) NoDerog/iStockphoto, (check) sjlocke/iStockphoto, (credit card) pagadesign/iStockphoto, (debit card) RTimages/Shutterstock, (dollar) jaanall/Fotolia, (twenty dollar) schankz/Fotolia, (quarter) bennyartist/Fotolia, (dime) mattesimages/Fotolia, (quarters) haveseen/Shutterstock, (ten dollar) acilo/iStockphoto, (dime) mattesimages/Fotolia, (nickel) rsooll/Fotolia, **97** (bl) ©Thinkstock, (br) ©sheff/Shutterstock, (bc) ©michaeljung/Shutterstock, **98** (cr) ©Norman Pogson/Shutterstock, (bl) ©Ilene MacDonald/Alamy, **99** (bl) ©Juice Images/Alamy, (tl) ©Monkey Business Images/Shutterstock, (tc) ©Inspirestock Inc./Alamy, (tr) ©CandyBox Images/Shutterstock, (bc) ©Deklofenak/Shutterstock, (br) ©White Packert/The Image Bank/Getty Images, **101** (tl) ©Jeroen van den Broek/Shutterstock, (tc) ©Pressmaster/Shutterstock, (tr) ©Huntstock/Getty Images, (bl) ©ARENA Creative/Shutterstock, (bc) ©Jupiterimages/Getty Images, (br) ©Diego Cervo/Shutterstock, **103** (tc) ©David Zaitz/Alamy, **111** (tl) ©Blend Images/Alamy, (tc) ©bikcriderlondon/Shutterstock, (tr) ©moodboard/Alamy, (br) ©diego cervo/Fotolia, (bc) ©Jaume Gual/Getty Images, (bl) ©Tetra Images/Alamy, **117** (tl) ©Peter Zijlstra/Shutterstock, (tc) ©mihalec/Shutterstock, (tr) ©Daniel Loiselle/iStockphoto, (cl) ©Richard Peterson/Shutterstock, (c) ©Volodymyr Krasyuk/Shutterstock, (cr) ©Mike Flippo/Shutterstock, (bl) ©Margo Harrison/Shutterstock, (bc) ©R. Gino Santa Maria/Shutterstock, (br) ©Odua Images/Shutterstock, **123** (tl) ©Jupiterimages/Getty Images/Thinkstock, (tc) ©Fancy/Alamy, (tr) ©Cultura Creative/Alamy, (bl) ©Jim David/Shutterstock, (bc) ©Jupiterimages/Getty Images/Thinkstock, (br) ©iStockphoto/Thinkstock, **129** (tl) ©Brandy Taylor/iStockphoto, (tc) ©Enigma/Alamy, (tr) ©B. Leighty/Photri Images/Alamy, (cl) ©muzsy/Shutterstock, (c) ©iofoto/Shutterstock, (cr) ©Andreas Gradin/Shutterstock, (bl) ©cassiede alain/Shutterstock, (bc) ©Profimedia.CZ a.s./Alamy, (br) ©IM_photo/Shutterstock, **130** (tr) ©Wirepec/Fotolia, **131** (tr) ©idreamphoto/Shutterstock, (tcr) ©iStockphoto/Thinkstock